You Don't Have

To Be A Kid

To Pull A

Rabbit Out Of A Hat

Magic For Adults

You Don't Have

To Be A Kid

To Pull A

Rabbit Out Of A Hat

Magic For Adults

Paul Daniels &Barry Murray

Barricade Books Inc.

Published by Barricade Books Inc.
150 Fifth Avenue
Suite 700
New York, NY 10011

Photography: John Lilley
Editor: Antonia Owen
Design: Richard Souper

Library of Congress Cataloging-in-Publication Data

Daniels, Paul.
    (Paul Daniels adult magi c)
    You don't have to be a kid to pull a rabbit out of a hat: magic
    For adults/ Paul Daniels & Barry Murray.
        p.   cm.
    Originally published under the title: Paul Daniels adult magic.
    London: Michael O'Mara Books, 1989
      ISBN: 1-56980-119-3
        1. Conjuring. I. Murray, Barry.   II. Title
    GV1547.D16 1997   97-17778
    793.8-dc21   CIP

Printed in the United States of America

10 9 8 7 6 5 4 3 2 1

This one's for Lou

CONTENTS

GLOSSARY

Block of cards: In which a number of cards are kept together during shuffling, cutting or dealing.

Cut: In which the pack is divided. The top half of the pack is cut off and the cut is completed when the bottom half of the pack is placed on top of the original top half.

Deal: In which single cards are dealt from the pack held in a dealing position.

Effect: What the trick is perceived to be by the spectator.

Face card: The only visible card, either on the bottom of the pack or on a small packet, when the cards are squared up in alignment.

False shuffle: In which the cards are apparently mixed into a random order, whilst being retained in their original order.

Fan: In which the cards are evenly spread in a fan-like display for exhibition or selection.

Flourish: A visual demonstration of skill or dexterity.

Force: In which the magician causes a spectator to choose a particular card or object whilst apparently being given a free choice. Also known as Hobson's Choice or Magician's Choice.

Glimpse: To secretly see and note a card or number.

Gimmick: Any magical prop or artefact or component which has been secretly prepared in advance and is used as an aid to making a trick work. The audience is never aware of the existence of this prepared item.

Indice: The numeral, letter or pip in the corners of the face of a playing-card identifying its suit, value or characteristic.

Indifferent cards: Those cards which are unimportant to the effect and method during the performance of a trick.

Key card: A known card which locates or marks the position of selected cards or stacks or set-ups.

Key number: The essential number that makes any mathematical formula work as the basic principle of a trick.

Locate: To find or establish the position of a card in the pack.

Mechanic's grip: A favoured method of holding the deck by card sharps and magicians which facilitates false deals or secret manoeuvres.

Misdirection: The means, whether physical or psychological, by which the magician diverts the spectator's attention away from a secret move or aspect of a trick.

Move: The specific technique, skill or manoeuvre executed by the magician to achieve the effect.

Overhand shuffle: A standard method of mixing a pack of cards.

Packet: Any small number of cards held in alignment.

Palm: To secretly conceal some small object, such as a coin or gimmick, in the hand.

Patter: The words spoken by the performer during the performance of a trick.

Practice: The development of an automatic facility, by repetition, of technique, skill and ability to a point of certainty in actual performance.

Presentation: The overall performance of a trick.

Props: The actual physical properties required for a trick. For example, a pack of cards is a prop.

Ribbon spread: The even distribution of an overlapping spread of cards in a row on the table.

Riffle shuffle: An on-the-table shuffle in which the two halves of the pack are interwoven as the thumbs riffle up and release the cards singly at speed.

Showmanship: The essential aspect of presentation. The means of selling, in a theatrical and performance sense, the effect and yourself. An innate ability with the great stars.

Sleight: A secret move or manoeuvre which in part or whole accomplishes the effect.

Stack: An arrangement of cards in a known or pre-determined sequence.

Stock: A group of cards which may be controlled.

Square up: To neatly assemble the cards into alignment.

Talon: The block of cards remaining after the removal of a small portion or cards.

Undercut: The opposite of a standard cut in that the bottom half of the pack is cut onto the top half of the pack.

Waterfall shuffle: A showy, in-the-hands shuffle which could also be categorized as a flourish.

X'ing the cut: Placing the cut cards at right-angles across the tabled cards. It is also used as a card force.

INTRODUCTION

Most introductions serve to provide the author's general preamble on the theme, content and background of the book's given subject. However, because this is a magic book, I'm going to break with tradition by immediately giving you a little hands–on experience. All you need is a banknote and two trombone-style paper-clips **1**.

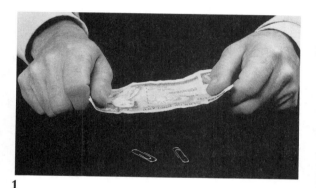

1

Hold the note by each end, bring your right hand over your left and clip the edges of the note together near your left thumb **2**. Then

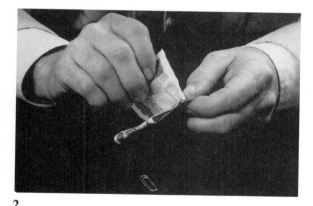

2

bring your right hand back and clip the top and middle edges together near your right thumb. So now you've folded a sort of S shape with the top and middle edges clipped together at the right-hand end and the middle and bottom edges clipped together at the left-hand end **3**.

With a brisk snap, pull the banknote straight.

3

4

The paper-clips will pop off the note. And as sure as my name is Paul Daniels, they'll be linked together **4**.

Congratulations. You have just done your first magic trick. Welcome to Wonderland. Actually you have achieved considerably more than your first trick. You have set up the trick by interpreting these instructions off the page. You have exercised your brain a little in doing so. You have occupied a little of your time in self-amusement. You may even be a little intrigued. How does it work? You know that clipping the note together at different points is a factor, and the action of quickly pulling the note straight forces the paper-clips off the note resulting in their linking. So what happens technically? It must belong to a specific area of knowledge. But which one and in what category? Where does it come from anyway? Did somebody invent it? And wouldn't it be a good idea to show it to your friends. But you'll want to practise it first, because you won't want them to be able to reconstruct it immediately and do it themselves. You want it to be your secret, so you can show it to lots of people. By then you'll be performing it just like a real magician, interacting with people. So what will you talk about as you do it? You'll need to think of something interesting to say. And if you can do all this with a banknote and two paper-clips, what could you do with a pack of cards? There's more to this magic business than deceives the eye, isn't there?

The trick you have just done became widely popular in magic circles after its publication in a specialist conjurors' magazine, *The New Phoenix*, in June 1954. Its creator was Bill Bowman of Seattle, Washington. It is categorized as a topological trick. Topology is a branch of mathematics that investigates the properties of a geometric configuration (as a set point) that are unaltered if the configuration is subjected to a one-to-one continuous transformation in both directions – in other words, the study of changing shapes. What specifically happens during the trick is a transference of the curves in the banknote to the paper-clips so that they link together **5**.

5

If you are beginning to think this is all rather heavy-going, a quick dip into Chapter 6 will ease your fears. Look up 'Juggle' – that's fun. And I recommend Chapter 4 for some very interesting items. In fact I recommend all the chapters, because I recommend magic. This book represents the tip of a magical iceberg that can have an impact on your life you wouldn't believe possible. But isn't that what magic is all about? The more you read this book, the more tricks you learn from it, the more sheer pleasure you'll gain for yourself and you'll give to others.

Enjoy.

Paul Daniels.

CHAPTER 1
WHY MAGIC?

The best effect of any book is that it excites the reader to self-activity.
— *Thomas Carlisle*

Why not? All sorts of people do magic. It's one of the most fascinating, interesting and stimulating subjects you could possibly find.

What is your perception of magic? Do you see it as something beyond your capabilities? Or is it that you just don't know where to begin?

Well, the moment you opened this book you made a start, for magic is entirely within your capabilities. All you need is some help and encouragement, and that's easily arranged.

On any evening the world-famous Magic Circle is open to its members, you could find an MP swapping card tricks with a solicitor who, in turn, learned much of his technique from a British Rail employee. Some of the most esteemed men and women in magic are amateur magicians. Many of the greatest effects in magic, whether small close-up tricks carried in the pockets, cabaret miracles or full-size stage illusions, were invented by amateur magicians. And the vast majority of magicians in the world of magic are amateurs, men and women who pursue the subject as a hobby whilst spending their working lives holding down a regular job. They don't sound a whole lot different to you, do they? What they get from their interest in the subject is one particular,

Paul doesn't recommend this particular trick for the amateur.

massive benefit – an antidote to the stresses of modern life. Magic is a rich subject; its history is over five thousand years old. It is a performance art, adaptable to any situation. It has a wealth of published specialist literature. Its appeal is universal; a trick that baffles a German will have the same effect on a Peruvian Indian. There is something in magic for everybody, and it's a marvellously sociable activity.

Look at this array of names: Charles Dickens, Lewis Carroll, F. Scott Fitzgerald, Vladimir Nabokov, Orson Welles, Cary Grant, Tony Curtis, Johnny Carson, Dick Cavett, Lord Mountbatten, Prince Charles, Winston Churchill, Albert Einstein, Muhammed Ali, Michael Jackson, James Stewart, Harold Lloyd. The list could continue indefinitely. All these people were or are active magicians or fascinated by the subject, with good reason.

Most people assume that magic is a very difficult subject to get into. This popular misconception is probably nurtured by the prevailing belief that magicians as a body are highly secretive people who would rather die an agonizing death than reveal a secret, letting nothing slip even under the most extreme duress.

Nothing could be further from the truth. Every trick, every secret method and principle has been published and is in print. How else can people become magicians and sustain their interest, without access to the literature of magic, this enormous treasure-house of material. Magicians have been exposing their secrets to the general public in books for centuries. The popular weekly and monthly magazines of the late Victorian and early Edwardian period were undoubtedly the seed-bed that published much of the magic we categorize today as public domain. Books and pamphlets flourished, often attracting would-be purchasers by their lurid covers. Note the price of the example illustrated here, published over sixty years ago.

So, you see, it's always been possible to get involved in magic. And the real secret, the one magicians don't publicize too much, is that magic is fun. So now you know, come and join us. It could prove to be the best move you ever make. And don't sidetrack yourself with that catch-all of an excuse, 'I'm a busy person. I just don't have the time.' Look at that list of names again. Aren't they busy people? They made the time. Work your way through this book and you'll find out why.

CHAPTER 2
ANTI-STRESS PLAY MAGIC

The mind ought sometimes to be amused,
that it may the better return to thought,
and to itself. – *Phaedrus (fifth century BC)*

Stress occurs when the tasks in everyday life begin to become a burden and the demands upon you exceed your ability to cope with them. This definition was given by Carol Hampton of Energy Unlimited. A professional stress counsellor, she maintains that taking a little time during the day to divert the mind away from the immediate problems confronting it can be enormously beneficial.

I don't suggest for one second that you regress to childhood, but I do advocate the pleasure and stimulus of intellectual play magic as an energizing alternative to more time-consuming pursuits.

THE IRISH COMPASS

This is a classic pocket magic trick, popularly known to magicians as the Chinese Compass. Its origins as an optical effect seem to be rooted in a 'line on block' novelty sold by pitchmen travelling with street carnivals in the United States during the early years of this century. Its application to magic during the 1930s and 1940s are credited, independently, to Val Evans and Evan Morgan; since when it grew like Topsy.

Here is an amusing version that is easy to prepare, easy to handle, easy to present and, not least, easy to practise. If you can do a passable Irish accent, your presentation will be all the more entertaining.

The Effect
The magician removes a small octagonal piece of card from his pocket and demonstrates that it is in fact a compass.

'The Irish are very clever people, you know. Look at this – it's the sort of compass they use in remote country regions to get about. You see it has an arrow on both sides, both pointing the same way. Even if you point it in the opposite direction, both arrows point the same way. And that's how it works for the Irish. As long as they follow the direction the arrow is pointing in, they'll always get to where they go. Now you couldn't have anything more Irish than that, to be sure.

'However, as you probably know, the Irish are reputed to be fond of a drop of the hard stuff, the water of life, the poteen, the imbibing of which can play a merry dance with one's equilibrium. Which is where the compass comes in, you see, after a convivial night spent toasting the memories of absent friends and all the blesssed saints, plus an essential three for the road. You point the arrow to the north if you want to get to the east. Did you follow that? Look, I'll show you again. Pointing it to the north guarantees the way to get to the East.

'But if it's south you're wanting to go, you'll get there a lot quicker by going west. Of course if you wanted to go thisaway, you wouldn't be going thataway. For sure, this-away is the opposite way to thataway. Are you following this? If you were Irish you would be. But the wonderful thing about the Irish Compass is that no matter where you go, there you are. And very often you'll end up where you've been, which is where you started. Which is the place where the poteen is poured. And by now you'll be sober again from all the exercise you've taken. So you'll convince yourself you're deserving of a glass or two. And you'll not worry about getting home late. For sure, you've got the Irish Compass safely in your pocket to get you there.'

The Secret

The secret is in the construction. Look at the exploded diagram **1** and then at the made-up compass. It's easily made from a piece of card **2**. When correctly prepared, the front and back arrows will be at right-angles to each other. So, provided you learn and practise the routine in conjunction with your patter, the effect will work automatically for you.

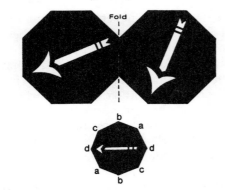

1

2

3

Look at the second photograph and play with the compass by holding it between your fingers at different points. Turning it over, you will see how optically deceptive it is **3**.

Here is the sequence of handling and moves in relation to your performance and patter.

1. 'Look at this – it's the sort of compass . . .'
   Take the compass from your top outer breast pocket.
2. 'You see it has an arrow on both sides, both pointing the same way.'
   Hold the compass at points A, with the arrow pointing at your left shoulder. Turn it over with your finger several times.
3. 'Even if you point it in the opposite direction . . .'
   Turn the compass round 180 degrees clockwise, so the arrow is pointing in the opposite direction.
4. '. . . both arrows point the same way.'
   Hold it between finger and thumb at points A and turn it over with your finger several times.
5. 'You point the arrow to the north . . .'
   Hold the compass at points D with the arrow pointing straight up, towards your chin.
6. '. . . if you want to get to the east.'
   Turn it over once with your left finger. The arrow will be pointing to your left.
7. 'Look, I'll show you again. Pointing it to the north . . .'
   Turn it round 45 degrees anti-clockwise. You will be holding it at points D, the arrow pointing up towards your chin.
8. '. . . guarantees the way to get to the east.'
   Turn it over once with your left finger. The arrow will be pointing to your left.
9. 'But if it's South you're wanting to go . . .'
   Turn it round 45 degrees clockwise so that the arrow is pointing to the floor, holding it at points D **4**.
10. '. . . you'll get there a lot quicker by going west.'
    Turn it over once with your left finger. The arrow will be pointing to your right **5**.
11. 'Of course if you wanted to go thisaway . . .'

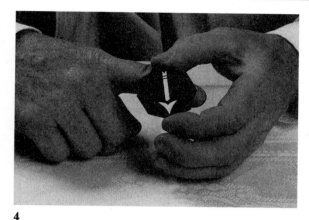

4

Turn it round clockwise 22½ degrees. And hold it at points C. The arrow will be pointing at your right shoulder.

12. '. . . you wouldn't be going thataway.'
    Turn it over once with your left finger. The

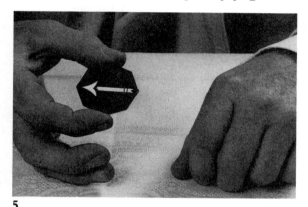

5

arrow will be pointing at your left foot.

13. 'For sure, thisaway . . .'
    Turn it over once with your left finger. The arrow will be pointing at your right shoulder.
14. '. . . is the opposite way to thataway.'
    Turn it over once with your left finger. The arrow will be pointing at your left foot.
15. 'And very often you'll end up where you've been . . .'
    Turn it round 45 degrees, so you're holding it at points A. The arrow will be pointing at your left shoulder.
16. '. . . which is where you started.'
    Turn it over once with your left finger.
17. 'Which is the place where the poteen is poured.'
    Keep turning it over.

18. '. . . from all the exercise you've taken.'
    Stop turning the compass over.
19. 'For sure, you've got the Irish Compass safely in your pocket . . .'
    Put it back into your top outer breast pocket.

I will emphasize three points, because they are important. Turning the compass over creates the effect; turning it round clockwise or anti-clockwise precedes and sets up the effect; and, of course, you will perform throughout facing the spectator.

If you make up a second, straight compass on which both arrows are pointing the same way to the same point D and keep it in your top pocket, you could switch your performance compass for the straight compass quite easily. After seeing the trick, spectators may well ask to see the compass for themselves. Reach into your top pocket and take out the second, straight compass and hand it to them. A full description and variation of this switch is explained using playing-cards on page 148.

Given the straight compass which produces no effect, the spectator can only wonder at the mystery of the Irish Compass. He might even begin to think he'd had a drop too much of the hard stuff himself.

FOOTNOTE

An amusing footnote to this routine is the following true story. In 1977 Paul was performing in Dublin. As his days were free, not having to arrive at the theatre until the early evening, he decided he would go for a drive in the beautiful Irish countryside. Some hours later he returned to his hotel a little the worse for wear. Feeling rather fraught, he went to the hotel lounge for a reviving cup of tea. The waiter, a friendly soul, inquired about Paul's day.

'Well,' said Paul, 'the country is beautiful but there was one problem. I was worried I was going to be late getting back for tonight's show because there were no signposts or road signs anywhere. It must be a real problem for you getting about.'

'Oh no, sir, no problem at all,' the waiter replied.

'No problem?' Paul asked. 'How's that?'

The waiter smiled. 'Well, you see, sir, we know where we're going.'

ONE TO FOUR COUNTDOWN

This intriguing magic puzzle will keep people amused for ages and, in same cases, baffled for ever.

Lay out ten coins of any denomination head side up in a circle on the table, so the edges of each coin are not touching **1**. The object of the

1

puzzle is to turn nine coins tail side up **2**. The rules of the puzzle are that players must start on a head and finish on a head and progress by counting in fours, tapping one coin consecutively for each number from one to four. The fourth coin is then turned over, tail side up. The

2

players can count by going clockwise or anti-clockwise, starting anywhere. They can't leap-frog; they must count consecutively. They can't start or finish on a tail, but they can include them in the count at numbers two and three in order to progress the count.

The unusual aspect of this puzzle is that in order to show them what the rules are, you actually complete the puzzle. As the puzzle can only be successfully completed by using a secret sequence, they actually see you do it but don't recognize it. Unless you know it, it's impossible to follow.

Before reading the solution, try doing it as the spectators would, in order to appreciate what a tough little cookie this is.

Solution

Starting anywhere, count one–two–three and turn the fourth coin tail up. The second count you start so that you finish on the coin that you started your first count on. The third count you start so that you finish on the coin you started your second count on. And so on. It's beautifully simple. The fact that you vary the count clockwise and anti-clockwise as you wish is what makes this so hard to follow even when demonstrated. It's also a very nice item for the card table. Lay out two rows of five cards face down. The puzzle is to turn nine of the ten cards face up. The same rules and the same solution apply.

THE SEVEN DEADLY SINS

The objective of this seemingly simple puzzle is to cover each deadly sin with seven pennies, leaving the No Sins circle uncovered.

You start by placing a coin on any of the eight circles. You must then move the coin to another circle along one of the straight lines. For example, if you start by placing a coin on Ire, you must then move the coin along one of the lines leading from it. So you make a choice between moving to Lechery or Envy.

Whichever one you cover, the coin must remain there.

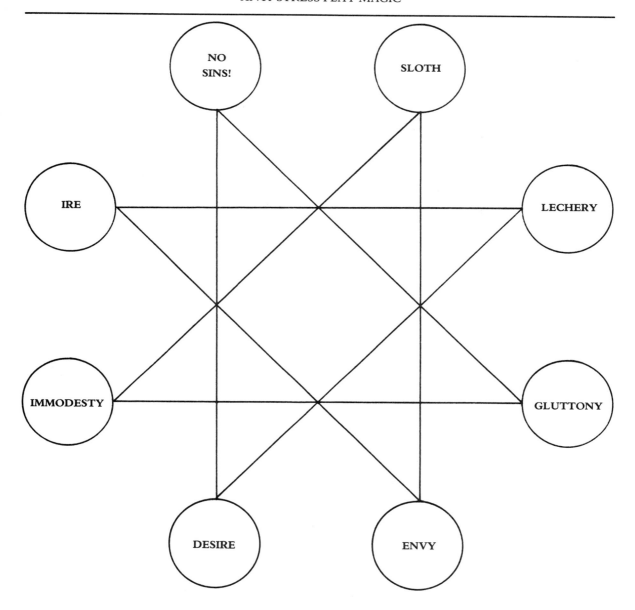

You cannot start from the same circle twice. You cannot start from a circle that is already covered by a coin. No coin can move more than once. As you progress, you will suddenly come to a point where you can't make another move. It will be interesting to see what deadly sin you get stuck on.

The puzzle can done, so don't rush to look up the solution. The fun is in the sense of achievement you get when you solve it. When you do, you can give it to your friends to try and watch them struggle.

Solution

Here is the set sequence of moves that solves this amusing puzzle. You put a coin on Start and move it to Finish and leave it there.

	Start		Finish
First coin:	Lechery	move to	Desire
Second coin:	Ire	move to	Lechery
Third coin:	Envy	move to	Ire
Fourth coin:	Sloth	move to	Envy
Fifth coin:	Immodesty	move to	Sloth
Sixth coin:	Gluttony	move to	Immodesty
Seventh coin:	No sins!	move to	Gluttony

RON:
A DIVERSION

Paul's diagram shows how easily it fits a business card.

One day late into the evening in the Seek-and-Find Division of NASA, a solitary programmer named Ron decided to bench test a prototype model of a new generation of megachip computers with an impossible question. 'What is the secret of life?' he typed on the keyboard. This amused Ron. There was no answer to that. There was a moment of silence as the computer's memory attempted to process the question.

Suddenly the VDU monitor blipped and the word HARMONY appeared.

Ron was surprised and puzzled by this response. He decided to ask another question. He punched it in slowly and deliberately with one finger. 'PROVE IT.'

This time the computer's response was instantaneous. 'ENTER YOUR NAME,' the display commanded.

Still puzzled but now intensely curious, Ron entered his name.

Instantly a small bright star appeared in the centre of the screen and then the letter O around the star. Then either side of the O with the star in it, the letters RN appeared. 'Hello, Ron,' said the computer. FIG. 1.

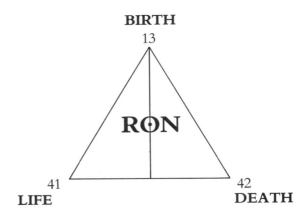

FIG. 1

Ron was astonished, it wasn't programmed to speak! It didn't have a synthesized voice chip!

The computer spoke again. 'The sum of human existence is birth, life and death. Do you agree?'

'Uh, yes,' Ron responded apprehensively.

As he spoke a triangle appeared on the monitor, enclosing his name. Then the word BIRTH above the apex of the triangle, followed by LIFE at the lower left point and DEATH at the right point. 'Ron. Give me any number of your choice,' the computer requested.

Ron, who was tempted to pull the plug, decided to play along. 'Thirteen,' Ron replied. He was born on a thirteenth so it was a lucky number for him. But the computer wouldn't know that, Ron thought smugly.

The numerals 13 appeared under the word BIRTH on the monitor. Ron frowned. 'Give me any number that you wish to represent life.'

'Forty-one,' Ron murmured, giving his age.

The numerals instantly appeared on the screen over the word LIFE. 'Any number to represent death.'

Ron's family were noted for their longevity. He had a reasonable expectation and every intention of being around for many, many more years. 'Forty-two,' he said flatly.

The number appeared over DEATH on the monitor, followed by a bright circle around the triangle, the circumference touching each point of the enclosed triangle. 'This is the circle of life,' stated the computer. 'Add the numerals of birth and life.'

Ron entered 13 plus 41 into the computer. The number 54 appeared inside the circle and the line of the triangle.

'Add the numerals of life and death.'

Ron entered 41 plus 42. With two audible blips the figures 83 appeared in the space between the line and the curve.

'Add the numerals of death and birth.'

Ron entered 42 plus 13. The number 55 inevitably appeared in the appropriate space. FIG. 2. What now? Ron wondered.

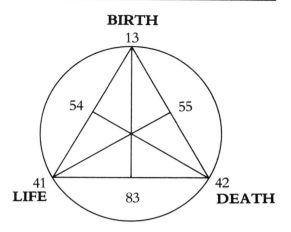

FIG. 3

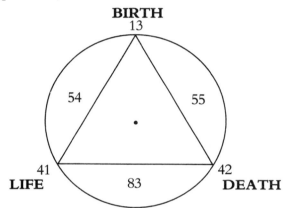

FIG. 2

Nothing happened. Ron was aware of the distant, muted hum of working computers. Somewhere else a door hissed open and shut. He stared at the screen and sighed heavily. 'Is that it? Just a graphic?' he said aloud, with mild disgust.

Instantly three lines lasered across the triangle, dissecting it from each point to exactly half-way along the line between the other points of the triangle to where the sums of the numerals were displayed. The lines crossed at the star in the centre of the graphic image. FIG. 3.

'This is your life, Ron,' said the computer.

Ron was staggered. Is it trying to be funny? he wondered. It *can't* have a sense of humour! But then it can't speak either, but it is. Ron

began to feel queasy. Then he began to feel uneasy. He looked around. There was no one else on the floor. He was alone. His nerves began to tingle. What to do? Maybe if I . . .

The computer interrupted his thoughts. 'Here is the proof. Add the numbers at the opposite end of each connecting line.'

Ron wanted to run, but the compulsion was too strong. His hand shook as he entered 13 + 83, and 41 + 55 and finally 42 + 54. Even

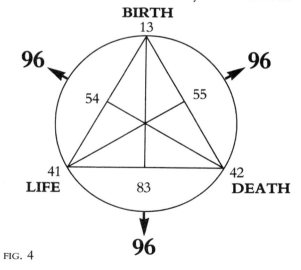

FIG. 4

as the numbers appeared, 96, 96, 96, he knew the real answer! It was a revelation! FIG. 4. The secret of life is subjective. It's the number of years you live. In his case ninety-six years. He was euphoric, ecstatic. He knew! Everything being equal the answer *was* Harmony.

Security found him early the next morning, giggling and standing on his head. He had inked the number 96 on his forehead.

'See,' he told the astonished guards as they took him away. 'It's the same, no matter which way you look at it. Ninety-six. It's the secret of life. Don't you see?'

Ron was put on indefinite sick-leave and was never aware of a conversation that took place a week later at an IBM Research and Development Program Division over a thousand miles away.

'Hey, Aero,' Loudstein yelled across the room of Department B20. 'There's another one.'

Aaron Liebeschnitz clenched his jaw muscles in annoyance. He was busy programming one of his little mathematical games deep into the computer's memory. The games were designed to divert and frustrate would-be hackers from retrieving classified information. But he regarded them also as aesthetic niceties, almost like his own personal signature tune.

'Hey, Aero, did you hear what I said?' Loudstein's penetrating voice cut across the room.

Liebeschnitz resented the intrusion into his concentration, but he knew from experience that Loudstein wouldn't give up until he was acknowledged. 'Another what?' he asked, as he turned to glare pointedly at Loudstein.

It was lunchtime. Loudstein always had the same routine. He read the daily paper as he stuffed his face. One day he'll choke on it, thought Liebeschnitz. The idea pleased him.

'It says here,' said Loudstein, through a mouthful of hero sandwich, 'another tester's gone loopy at NASA. Working on one of your HALs.'

'So, what does that prove?' asked Liebeschnitz with defensive irritation.

'You kidding me?' said Loudstein. 'That's the third one this month. I told you that it was a mistake to christen this series HAL.'

'Nonsense,' snorted Liebeschnitz, 'It was just a little in-joke for sixties survivors. My HAL means HArmonious Life.'

'Some joke!' Loudstein retorted.

'Well, I wouldn't expect you to see the funny side,' Liebeschnitz bristled. 'It's far too subtle for you.'

As the exchange continued and the temperature of the argument increased, both men were far too preoccupied to notice the words HARMONY LIVES flash on to the monitor of Liebeschnitz's computer. The words had long faded by the time Liebeschnitz turned and stared at the blank screen of the monitor. I really must complain about Loudstein, he thought. These constant interruptions. One of these days I'll make a mistake.

It isn't necessary to relate the story to present this mathematical novelty. Using the Birth, Life and Death theme and personalizing it with the spectator's name – or initial if it's a long name – should be sufficient, especially if you present it as a means of finding a spectator's lucky life number. Draw it on your business card and leave it with them. Limit their choice of numbers from nought to one hundred. Most of us live and die within that span, even magicians.

CHAPTER 3
SALES MAGIC

To be a success in business, be daring, be first, be different. – *Marchant*

If you are in business, you are in the business of selling yourself. This means getting people to notice you, to remember you, to want to see you in preference to the other person.

So what have you got that's different? You're the one who does magic, the one who doesn't present the same old predictable pitch. You're the one they're pleased to see.

Think about it. They'll give you more time, because you break up their day in an original and acceptable way. You have personalized your approach the magic way. It induces a response.

They're having fun, they're relaxed and more receptive to what you came to say. Magic can give you the edge over your competitors and that's worth its weight in gold.

PAUL'S PUZZLE BOX

Ask a friend if he has a penny on him. Instruct him to hold it by the edges between his thumb and forefinger and to study the illustration.

Tell him you are going to test his perception. Does he think he can lay the coin on the box without it touching the printed lines? Most people would bet that they could. In fact it's impossible. It's a very deceptive optical illusion.

Being a magician, there is, of course, a pretty sneaky way in which you can do it. Repeat the conditions of the test but use the word 'place' instead of 'lay', because that's exactly what you do. You place the coin in the box by standing it on edge. It's a nice little quickie to have on the back of your business card.

SPIRIT CARD

1

Business cards are such a fact of commercial life it's surprising there is so little really good magic making use of them. Here is a super spooky trick to help remedy the situation **1**.

The Effect
The magician shuffles a pack of cards and has a spectator cut the pack. The top half of the pack is placed at a right-angle across the bottom half to mark where the spectator cut.

Taking his business card from his wallet, the magician points to the plain white back of the card and says, 'This may look like a plain card to you. But in fact it is a means of contacting the spirit world. Do you believe in spirits?' The spectator will probably answer no. Undaunted, the magician continues. 'Do you believe in the spirit of increased market share?' The spectator may concede the possibility. 'Do you believe in the great spirit of doubling your profits 100 per cent over year ending forecasts? Yes, of course you do. I'll ask you one final vital question. Do you believe in magic?' Whatever the response, the magician concludes, 'Well, you should. Let's see if the spirits have been satisfied with your answers.'

The magician rubs a pencil over the back of the card and slowly the letters of a playing-card appear, 7H – the seven of hearts. 'Let's see the card you cut to.' The magician turns the card over to reveal the seven of hearts. 'You have truly found favour with the spirits!'

2

The Secret

Put the seven of hearts on top of the pack. You will find it easy enough to riffle shuffle the cards, retaining the seven of hearts on top, by keeping it back with your right thumb and only releasing it after all the cards in your left hand have been released.

Get a bar of white soap and cut a thick sliver from it. Then print the letters 7H on the blank back of a white business card with the edge of the soap. Don't make the letters too thick. Brush off any obviously visible bits of soap and put the card in your wallet top pocket. You're all set to go.

Choose a spectator and false shuffle the pack as described, keeping the seven of hearts on top. Holding the pack in your left hand, ask the spectator to cut the cards. He will cut off a portion of the cards; it doesn't matter how many. As soon as he cuts, immediately take the cards from him and put them on the table. Then, without pausing, take the remainder of the pack from your left hand and place it at a right-angle on top of the cards on the table, saying, 'We'll mark the cut.' **2** Then, without pausing, take the business card from your pocket, draw attention to it and go into your presentation. In fact you have forced the seven of hearts.

To reveal the letters on the business card, run the point of a soft dark coloured pencil shading

over and around the soap letters, which will slowly stand out in contrast to the graphite or crayon. Then pick off the top half of the pack and turn over the card on the bottom half to reveal their card, the seven of hearts **3**.

3

Bear in mind that the soap letters on your business card will dry and flake off if left for too long before use. So it would make sense to prepare a card and carry it for a while to gauge the length of its useful life. The reason for using the seven of hearts as a force card is that it's easy to write 7H with soap, because it is comprised of straight lines.

Attention to such small detail in preparation and sufficient practice are essential to the mechanics of good magic. The certainty of the physical aspect of a trick working allows the magician the essential peace of mind that enables him to concentrate on the presentation and performance of the trick.

NO CARDS MENTAL TEST

Welcome to the first card trick in the book, although you won't need a pack of cards. What you will need are two file cards, post-cards, or appropriately for this chapter, two business cards.

The Effect

The magician shows two cards on which are depicted a full pack of playing-cards, including jokers and bridge score cards. Handing the first card to a spectator, the magician turns his back and asks him to think of any card, even a joker or bridge score card, then to find it on the first card, clip a strip of paper over the column it is in and do the same on the second card.

The magician turns around and points out that, even though he can't see what cards are in the covered columns, if the spectator concentrates on his chosen card he will name it. This he immediately does!

The Secret

Because of its simplicity this is one of the best tricks in the book. It is very portable, easy to accomplish, and extremely baffling.

For the purpose of instruction we have marked our cards 1 and 2. When you make your cards up, it won't be necessary. If you study both cards you can easily distinguish between them by remembering that card number 1 has the KH in the top right-hand corner. And card number 2 has the 9S in the top right-hand corner. So KH = 1 and 9S = 2.

An even greater simplification is to remember that red equals card number 1 and black equals card number 2. As the king of hearts is a red colour, card number 1 is red. The nine of spades is black, so card number 2 is black. Even

if the spectator selects the king of hearts or any card in that column on card number 1 and covers it with a strip of paper, the nine of spades will be uncovered on card number 2. So at a glance you will know which card is which. The significance of this I'll explain shortly.

The most practical way to learn the trick is for you to do it using the diagrams and playing the dual role of magician and spectator.

Select *any* card on card number 1 (KH = red = 1) and clip a strip of paper over the length of the column the card is in, having first prepared two thin strips of paper just wide enough and long enough to cover completely a single column vertically. Then locate and cover the same card in the first column it appears in on card number 2 (9S = black = 2). Now we reach the real secret of the trick. Card number 2 carries a secret formula which will actually reveal the spectator's mentally selected card. All you have to remember is the following code:

Column 1 is linked to column 3
Column 2 is linked to column 4
Column 5 is linked to column 7
Column 6 is linked to column 8

In performance, when you get the cards back with columns covered, the trick works like lightning. Look at card number 2 and locate your 'key column'; for instance, if column 5 is covered, the code tells you column 7 is the key column and vice versa. Here's another example; if column 4 is covered, your key column is 2 and vice versa.

Now look at which column you have covered on card number 1. If it's column 2, look at the second card down in your key column on card 2. It will not be the chosen card but it will be the opposite of the chosen card. So it won't be difficult to work out. If you are looking at the three of diamonds, the selected card will be the three of hearts. The same applies to the black cards. The opposite of the jack of clubs is the jack of spades, etc. The only exceptions are jokers and score cards, which are straightforward opposites.

I'm sorry that this has taken a little explaining, because the calculation can be performed in a flash. Now try the trick a few times on yourself using the printed cards. To help you, here are the bare bones of the trick, from when you receive the two cards, with covered columns, from the spectator.

1. Locate key column on card number 2.
2. What number column is covered on card number 1?
3. Count down key column to that same number.
4. Note the card in that position. The opposite card is the chosen card.

One final tip to help you assimilate the coding formula on card number 2 is to remember the columns are linked by odd or even numbers – 1 and 3, 5 and 7; *or* 2 and 4, 6 and 8. Practise it for ten minutes a day for a week and it will be yours for life.

This is one of the few tricks that gains in mystery by repetition. You can even leave the cards with the spectator and he will not be able to figure out how to do it. If you have this trick printed on a gatefold-style business card or on two separate cards, I can guarantee that it will not be thrown away as so many others often are. If they remember this trick, they will remember you.

KC	3H	10S	5S	2D	10H	KH
JH	JC	4S	6D	AC	QD	8C
KS	3D	10C	5C	2H	10D	KD
JD	JS	4C	6H	AS	QH	8S
AH	QC	2S	9D	4H	8H	5H
9C	6S	7H	3C	J	7S	SC
AD	QS	2C	9H	4D	8D	5D
9S	6C	7D	3S	SC	7C	J

CARD No. 1

KC	JH	KS	JD	AH	9C	AD	9S
3H	JC	3D	JS	QC	6S	QS	6C
10S	4S	10C	4C	2S	7H	2C	7D
5S	6D	5C	6H	9D	3C	9H	3S
2D	AC	2H	AS	4H	J	4D	SC
10H	QD	10D	QH	8H	7S	8D	7C
KH	8C	KD	8S	5H	SC	5D	J

CARD No. 2

BRANDED TASTES

The power of advertising is such that the brand name and the product are often indivisible in the mass shopping psyche. Cornflakes are always Kellogg's Cornflakes, Beanz definitely do mean Heinz. And are there any colas other than Coke or Pepsi?

Here is a very effective trick that uses popular branded drinks.

The Effect

Showing ten of his business cards, the magician points out that on the back of each card is written the name of a popular drink with a sample stain of that drink **1**.

He cuts the cards a number of times, then offers the choice of one card from the face down spread **2**. A spectator takes any card of his choice and holds it face down. Closing the remainder of the cards, the magician feels

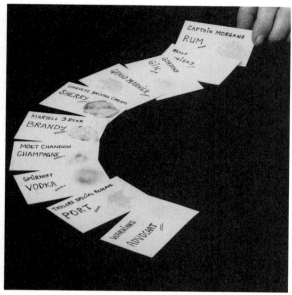

1

2

4. Grand Marnier
5. Sherry – Harveys Bristol Cream
6. Brandy – Martell Three Star
7. Champagne – Möet et Chandon
8. Vodka – Smirnoff
9. Port – Taylor's Special Reserve
10. Advocaat – Warnink's

Study this list for a while. Does it suggest anything to you, other than the desire for a large one. If you've answered 'No, nothing', you will appreciate the subtlety of the set-up. The brand names of the drinks are in alphabetical order. So stack and memorize the cards in order face down from 'Whisky – Bell's' on top, down to 'Advocaat – Warnink's' on the bottom, and then cut the cards a few times. You are now ready to try the trick on yourself for practice.

Fan the cards face down, take one out and put it face down on the table. Separate the cards at the place where you took a card and put the top right-hand portion under the bottom left-hand portion. In the process of squaring up the packet, fleetingly turn it towards you to see the name of the drink **3**. You will now know

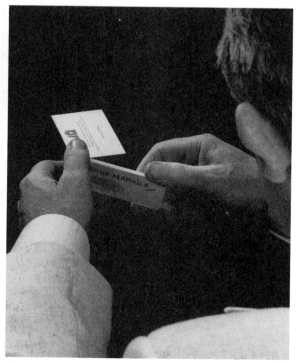

3

the underside of the spectator's card with a fingertip. He then touches his tongue with the fingertip. He deliberates for a moment as he samples the taste and then promptly announces the name of the drink. The card is turned over as 100 per cent proof that he is correct.

The Secret
On the backs of ten of your business cards write the names of each of the following drinks, in this order:

1. Whisky – Bell's
2. Rum – Captain Morgan's
3. Gin – Gordon's

that the chosen card is the one that follows the glimpsed card in the stacked alphabetical sequence.

As the cards are in a cyclic order, if the glimpsed bottom card is 'Whisky – Bell's', then 'Advocaat – Warnink's' is the card on the table. To put a little stain on each card, dip your finger into coffee, tea, cola, egg yolk, etc. and touch an appropriate card. If you want to go the whole way and stain each card with the appropriate drink, I'm sure your local off-licence will be pleased to see you.

To present the trick, you might patter on about the amount of entertaining you have done on the company's behalf over the years, to the extent that you can distinguish between drinks with the merest hint of a taste, without actually seeing, sniffing or drinking. So refined and sensitive are your tastebuds they cannot possibly fail to differentiate one drink from another. You then proceed to support these large claims by producing your cards and performing the trick. Presented as a connoisseur's demonstration, rather than a trick, it's very effective. Make a point of naming the drink first.

'It's sherry. Yes, sherry. Harveys Bristol Cream.' By pointing up the drinks and referring to the names as your favourite brands, nobody will notice the alphabetical order of the cards.

You can elaborate on this basic method. All ten drinks could be wines, the different regions and châteaux providing your stacked sequence. In knowledgeable company it could be an extremely strong effect, provided you only do it once or twice for the same audience.

THE MENTALIST

Mentalism is a specialist area of magic that demonstrates the mind-reading abilities of the magician. Some of the most puzzling feats in all magic derive from this source, possibly because there's almost nothing to be suspicious of. There is no flamboyant display of dexterity, there are no mysterious boxes or cabinets to wonder at, and there is no stunningly attractive assistant risking mutilation at the hands of a manic illusionist.

Usually the mentalist works from his pockets with common everyday articles, employing a blend of psychological insights and subtle magical principles to hoodwink his audience. Good mental magic packs a punch. Try this one and be convinced.

The Effect

We'll imagine the situation is one of a salesman visiting a prospective client. He offers a note-pad, on which are written some questions, to the client. The salesman requests that the client fills in the answers to the questions, without allowing the salesman to see the answers. But, before he begins writing, the salesman places his business card face up on the client's desk, with the comment, 'This may be significant later.' The client fills in the answers to the following questions, adds them all together and writes down the total.

Personal Questionnaire

1. Your year of birth
2. Your age at the end of the current year
3. The years you have been married
4. The year you were married

Total =

'I'm sure you will agree', the salesman continues, 'that I couldn't possibly know any of the individual figures that you've written or the total of their addition. Those figures are uniquely yours. And yet before I left my office to come here I wrote a prediction on the reverse of the sheet of notepaper you have just written on. Turn it over and you will find a four-figure number. Are those four figures the same as your questionnaire totals? They are! Isn't that amazing! But there's more to come. If you put a line in between the second and third figures, you split the four figures into two sets of two numbers. Now pick up the telephone directory that contains your surname. Turn to the page the first two figures indicate and then count down to the name and phone number entry the second two figures indicate. Have you done that? Please call them out loud. Now turn over my business card. There you see written the same name and phone number you have just called out. How could I possibly have known that in advance? If you find that surprising, just wait until I tell you what our products can do for you. This is where the real miracles come in.'

With this, our enterprising mentalist salesman delivers his pitch to the client, who, having been entertained in this unusual way, may be more receptive to the salesman's persuasion.

The Secret

The trick depends on the unusual and little-known mathematical fact that the total of the answers to the personal questionnaire will always be twice the current year.

This book was first published in 1989. So as an example we'll use Paul Daniel's personal questionnaire.

1. Your year of birth	1938
2. Your age at the end of the current year	51
3. The years you have been married	1
4. The year you were married	1988
Total	= 3,978

Divide the total by two. This equals 1,989. Your advance preparation is to write the figure 3,978 on the reverse of the unanswered questionnaire, then to find page 39 in your local telephone directory and count down to the seventy-eighth entry and write that name and phone number on the back of your business card. If there is more than one local directory, as in the case of Greater London, use the one that covers the first letter of the surname of the person you intend to perform the trick for. The only other advance information you need to know is that the person is married and is capable of remembering the relevant dates.

THE MARVELLOUS MAGIC SQUARE

Recreational mathematicians have long amused themselves with the seeming limitless vari-

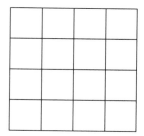

An example of the layout of a magic square before performance.

ations possible with the magic square. In over two thousand years it has not only been a subject of intellectual play but has been regarded as a source of mystical power by a variety of priests, astrologers, philosophers and artists to give credence to themselves or credibility to their respective offerings.

An interesting historical example of a symmetrical magic square of sixteen is seen in Albrecht Dürer's *Melencolia*. The engraving

Dürer's *Melencolia*.

was made in 1514, clearly evidenced in the second and third frames of the fourth horizontal row. An immediate understanding of the unusual properties of the square can be acquired by totalling the four numbers in each horizontal line, each vertical line, both diagonals, corner to corner, the four corner numbers, the four quarter frames of the square and the inner frame of four numbers. The total in each case is 34. The symbolic significance of the number 34

16	3	2	13
5	10	11	8
9	6	7	12
4	15	14	1

= 34

in relation to either Dürer, the engraving itself or melancholy in general has never been determined, although 34 is the lowest four-by-four square you can form with whole numbers.

Magicians have created many magic squares for the purpose of entertainment. Here are two of the very best.

'INSTANT SQUARE'

The Effect

The magician shows his business card. On the back of it he has drawn a square which has been divided into 16 smaller squares. Each square is blank. The magician asks a spectator to think of any number between 34 and 100. He holds the card and a pen as though in readiness to write. 'Tell us your number,' he says to the spectator. The magician instantly fills the squares on the card in a random manner, writing a series of numbers in no particular sequence. Within seconds, each frame in the square is filled. Handing the card to the spectator he asks him to total the four numbers in each vertical line, then the four numbers in each horizontal line, then the two diagonals, then the four numbers in each quarter of the frame, and so on in a seemingly never-ending combination. In each case the total arrived at is the same as the number the spectator thought of.

This demonstration cannot fail to impress your audience. They will credit you with an ability far beyond the minimal effort actually required to learn the technique.

The Secret

You have a choice of three ways of achieving the effect. The first, which is really the best, is to memorize the following square. There are only four numbers to calculate; the rest you write in exactly as illustrated in FIG. 1.

53 − 20 = Key number 33

K	1	12	7
11	8	K−1	2
5	10	3	K+2
4	K+1	6	9

FIG. 1

K is your key number, which you arrive at by subtracting 20 from the spectator's chosen number. For example, the spectator chooses 53. You subtract 20 from 53. This gives your key number of 33, which you write in the key frame on the first horizontal line.

In the key frame of the second horizontal line you write 32 (KEY number − 1). In the key frame of the third horizontal line you write 35 (K+2). And in the key frame of the fourth horizontal you write 34 (K+1).

Your completed square will look like this:

33	1	12	7
11	8	32	2
5	10	3	35
4	34	6	9

FIG. 2

You can now demonstrate the twenty-two different ways various numbers combine to total 53.

4 vertical lines
4 horizontal lines

2 diagonals	33	8	3	9
	4	10	32	7
11.	1	12	34	6
12.	11	5	35	2
13.	1	11	6	35
14.	12	2	5	34
15.	33	7	4	9
16.	33	1	11	8
17.	1	8	12	32
18.	12	7	32	2
19.	8	32	10	3
20.	5	10	4	34
21.	10	3	34	6
22.	3	6	35	9

If you don't wish to memorize the square, you could copy it on a piece of card small enough to be retained in your left hand, unseen by spectators but visible to you as you fill in the square on your business card, which your hand supports as you write. What you lose with this method is the opportunity to let the spectators actually see you filling in each frame.

Another method is to fill in each frame, apart from key numbers, beforehand very lightly with a soft lead pencil. If you write over the pencil figures with a reasonably thick felt-tip pen in performance, nobody should suspect any earlier preparation. The only risk is that some hawk-eyed spectator with twenty–twenty vision actually discerns the pencilled numbers.

The memory method is preferable, because you can do it instantly anywhere, any time. It's genuinely impromptu and it has the real advantage of allowing the spectators to see the numbers being written, which makes for a stronger presentation, especially if you fill in the squares haphazardly, in no obvious sequence. Ten minutes' practice daily for two weeks is all you'll need to add one of the most powerful tricks possible to your repertoire.

'LUCKY NUMBER SQUARE'

This novel presentation enables you to complete a magic square that totals a spectator's lucky number, even though you don't know what that number is.

Give a spectator a pen and notepad and ask him to write down any number between 34 and 70 that he feels is lucky for him, but not to let you see it. Then tell him to write your lucky number 90 under his number and add them together. Then he is to cross through the first digit on the left of his total and reposition it beneath the last digit on the right. Finally he is to add it to the number above it.

You point out that this new total bears no relation to his lucky number, as it is an entirely different number. He should agree. You then ask him to tell you this new total. As soon as he does you instantly fill in a sixteen-frame magic square on your business card. When it is completed you ask him to name aloud for the first time his original lucky number and proceed to demonstrate that the vertical lines, horizontal lines, diagonals, four corners, etc. all total his lucky number.

The Secret

When he has written his lucky number, for example, 46, on the notepad, you instruct him to write your lucky number, 90, underneath it and add them together.

$$\begin{array}{r} 46 \\ +90 \\ \hline 136 \end{array}$$ FIG. 1

Then to cross through the first digit on the left of his total and reposition beneath the last digit on the right and add them together.

$$\begin{array}{r} 46 \\ +90 \\ \hline 136 \\ +1 \\ \hline 37 \end{array}$$ FIG. 2

You ask him what this total is. As soon as he tells you, add 9 to it and you will have his original lucky number, 46.

$$\begin{array}{r} 46 \\ +90 \\ \hline \end{array}$$ FIG. 3

$$136$$
$$+1$$
———

$$37$$
$$+9$$
———

$$46$$　　FIG. 3

At this point the spectator has no idea that you actually know his lucky number, which makes the following magic square all the more amazing. FIG. 4. The first thing you do is

46–22 = Key number 24

1	14	K+3	4
K	7	6	9
8	K–1	10	5
13	2	3	K+4

FIG. 4

determine your key number, which you arrive at by subtracting 22 from his lucky number 46. This gives your key number 24, which you write in the key frame in the first vertical line. In the key frame of the second vertical line you write 23 (KEY number –1). In the key frame of the third vertical line you write 27 (KEY number +3). And in the key frame of the fourth vertical line you write 28 (KEY number +4).

Your completed square will look like this:

1	14	27	4
24	7	6	9
8	23	10	5
13	2	3	28

FIG. 5

With this square you can demonstrate twenty-four different combinations totalling 46.

4 vertical lines
4 horizontal lines
2 diagonals

1	7	10	28
13	28	6	4

11.	1	14	24	7
12.	27	4	6	9
13.	8	23	13	2
14.	10	5	3	28
15.	7	6	23	10
16.	14	24	5	3
17.	27	9	8	2
18.	24	8	9	5
19.	14	27	2	3
20.	1	4	13	28
21.	1	14	3	28
22.	27	4	13	2
23.	24	7	10	5
24.	6	9	8	23

If you actually add the numbers aloud as you demonstrate the various combinations, the presentation is stronger, particularly if you build up the tempo to arrive at a breathtaking climax with the last combination. Speed of presentation is what turns the magic square from a mathematical novelty into an astounding effect – all the more remarkable in this square because you, apparently, never knew the spectator's lucky number.

Another presentation of this square is to pick a spectator whose age you judge to be between 34 and 70. Ask him to write his age down, as opposed to his lucky number, and present it as a magic birthday square.

You can also preface your presentation of the magic square with a brief talk about numbers in general. How interesting, important and strange they are; how our lives are governed by them; people's shoe sizes, telephone numbers, house numbers, birth dates; superstitious numbers like 13 and the Devil's number, 666; one's bank account number; a very important number – our bank balance. Inflation is measured in numbers. In business the most important numbers of all are the figures on the bottom line. And the magic of numbers. Let me show you what I mean . . .

Try practising these squares with different numbers a couple of times a day for a week and you'll realize how direct and simple they are. But you probably won't appreciate how impressive they are to spectators until you present them. When you do, you will appreciate the marvellous magic square. Albrecht Dürer certainly did as long ago as 1514.

CHAPTER 4

A MAGICIAN IN THE OFFICE

Do you know that one–seventh of your entire life is spent on Mondays? – *Wizbit*

No one is suggesting you become the company conjuror, the resident court jester. But if you try some of these tricks you could interact with your office colleagues a lot better because of your ability occasionally to bring a little levity to the daily grind.

Magic will enhance your standing within the company. Good magicians are perceived as being clever people. Take advantage of this fact. Use it in sales presentations when you perform 'Just One of the Miracles We Do' for a client, talk about how 'we like to work with our clients, so we feel we're so in tune with their needs it's almost like we know what they're thinking'. Then hit them with the climax of the trick. It will have an impact. That's good for business, and that's good for you.

MEMO

Would you believe you could perform a stunning card trick for an associate in the office without either actually doing it or even being there? You should believe it, because in this book everything is possible, even the impossible.

The Effect

Picture this scene. It is four o'clock in the afternoon. A colleague in a different department receives the following items by internal messenger: a memorandum, a pack of playing-cards in its case and a sealed envelope on which is written, 'Read memo before opening.'

The memo reads as follows:

[your colleague's name]

[your name]

1. Place the sealed envelope to one side.
2. Remove the cards from their case.
3. Shuffle the pack.
4. Remove all the black spot cards below, not including, the value of four.
5. Remove all the red spot cards above, not including, the value of seven. No picture cards.
6. Put the bulk of the pack aside.
7. Pick up the small packets of red and black spot cards and thoroughly shuffle them together.
8. Place the packet face down on the table and look at the top card. This is now your chosen card. Remember it and turn it face down again on the packet.
9. Place the bulk of the pack face down on top of the small packet of cards.
10. You will agree I cannot possibly know the name of your card.
11. Pick up the pack and deal, one card at a time, twice as many cards as there are spots on your selected card.
12. Now turn over all the cards in your hand so they are face up and put them on top of the packet on the table.
13. Pick up the pack and deal another pile of cards on to the table by exercising the following choice:
    a) If your selected card is a spade or a heart deal twenty cards.
    b) If your selected card is a diamond or a club deal twenty-four cards.
14. Now again turn over the cards in your hand and put them on top of the pile on the table.
15. If you think the cards are getting messed up and mixed up, you're dead right.

16. Pick up the pack and make the following choice:
    a) If your card is a black card deal eighteen cards on to the table.
    b) If your card is a red card deal thirteen cards on to the table.
17. Turn the cards in your hand over and put them on top of the pile on the table.
18. You're getting the hang of this now, aren't you?
19. It's time for some magic. Pick up the pack. Now deal one card from the top of the pack on to the table for each letter of the following name: P-A-U-L D-A-N-I-E-L-S.
20. Now look at the top card of those in your hand.
21. That's magic!
22. Open the sealed envelope.

In the envelope is a second memo which reads:

To [your colleague's name]

From [your name]

It's just as well for the company that while you are goofing off playing with card tricks I'm taking care of business. PS Please return the pack.

The Secret

The trick is dependent on a very simple but well-disguised mathematical principle. Which is that whatever position the selected card is in from the bottom of the pack at the beginning of the trick, it will be the same numerical position from the top of the pack at the end of the trick. Now although the memo at stages 4 and 5 didn't specify the number of red and black cards to remove from the pack, a moment's thought will tell you that it had to be twelve. And that once he had memorized his selected card at stage 8, and then placed the bulk of the pack on top of the tabled packet at stage 9, his selected card was twelve up from the bottom of the pack.

The rest of the trick is just spoof and bluff. Words like 'choice' are used to convey a sense of exercising options, when in fact they dictate the movement of the selected card. Mixing up the pack in a seemingly random face-up, face-down way is a subtlety that misdirects him away from the progressive movement of the selected card. The simple fact is that whether the cards are face up or down there are still fifty-two cards in the pack – all that's necessary for a mathematical trick.

The significance of you forcing twelve cards, because that is what you have done in our example, is that there are eleven letters in Paul Daniels. So spelling and dealing one card on to the table for each letter guarantees the twelfth card will be the selected card. The beauty of this principle is that you can vary it and adapt it to suit the recipient's own name, or even a company name. For example, if you wanted to use the name Magic Marketing Ltd, you would write in the memo the instruction to remove all the black cards below the value of five (stage 4), then remove all the red cards above the value of five, excluding court cards (stage 5). This forces eighteen cards on the recipient. Do the rest of the trick as instructed and finally deal one card on the table for each letter of Magic Marketing Ltd. There are seventeen letters in the company name, so the eighteenth card will be the one he turns. It will also be his selected card.

The key to personalizing the trick is that the number of cards you force will always total one more than the number of cards spelt at the end.

If the name or message has twelve letters, then you can force thirteen cards by having the person deal the pack into four piles of thirteen cards. Look at and remember the top card of one pile, then put the other three piles on top of it.

You can do it over the phone or through the post, fax it or use a computer. You can spell names, company names, logos, etc. You are limited only by your imagination – which should be no limitation at all.

If the person uses his own pack, make sure he removes the jokers. You will have already done so if you send your own pack.

In a business context you could send a pack of cards and the instruction memo to clients as a Christmas promotional item. And you could even send one to the Managing Director of the company you work for, if he's got a sense of humour. If in doubt, send him a copy of this book instead!

£50 TO A PENNY

My introduction to part of this murderous proposition bet was through Martin Gardner, an unsung genius whose collective body of work contains an assembly of the most intelligent opinion and interesting ideas in the whole of magical literature. His books debunking many of our popular pseudo-sciences – and their equally pseudo practitioners – are particularly entertaining.

The Effect

You, the magician, tear a single match out of a book of paper matches and inks a line on one side of the match. You then tell a receptive colleague that by flicking the match into the air, 'like spinning a coin with my thumb', you can cause whichever side you want to land face up. Have him call 'Marked' or 'Unmarked' and flick the match into the air, declaring you will cause the opposite to happen. Whatever he calls he'll never get, because of your ability to control the match.

In fact this is pure bunkum designed to set him up for the real sting to follow. The odds are even, as which side of the match finishes face up is governed by pure chance every time. Some you'll win; some you'll lose.

You will probably suffer a little ribbing at your failure, which, of course, is what you want. Pretend to get irritated and say, 'All right. I'll tell you what we'll do. I bet you £50 that I can flick this paper match into the air and cause it to land on its edge and not on either side. If I fail, I'll give you a £50 note. If I succeed, you give me a single penny today, two pennies tomorrow, four the day after, and so on for thirty days only. So each successive day you give me twice as many pennies as you did the day before, for no longer than the month of November which has thirty days. I feel so certain I can do it I'll wager my £50 against your pennies.'

Needless to say, you will win the bet. The match indeed lands on its edge! What will not be quite so obvious is how many pennies your colleague will eventually owe you.

The Secret

To ensure that the paper match will land on its

edge, simply bend it around your thumb into a C shape with your fingers just before flicking it into the air. The match will land on its edge as you said. But what you didn't state was the condition of the match when it landed.

Now we come to the £50 to a penny wager. Are you sitting comfortably? Good, then I'll ask you how many pennies you think you will have been paid at the end of thirty days? The answer is £10,737,418.23 worth! The following chart shows how it grosses up.

Day	Pennies paid	Total pennies accrued
1	1	1
2	2	3
3	4	7
4	8	15
5	16	31
6	32	63
7	64	127
8	128	255
9	256	511
10	512	1,023
11	1,024	2,047
12	2,048	4,095
13	4,096	8,191
14	8,192	16,383
15	16,384	32,767
16	32,768	65,535
17	65,536	131,071
18	131,072	262,143
19	262,144	524,287
20	524,288	1,048,575
21	1,048,576	2,097,151
22	2,097,152	4,194,303
23	4,194,304	8,388,607
24	8,388,608	16,777,215
25	16,777,216	33,554,431
26	33,554,432	67,108,863
27	67,108,864	134,217,727
28	134,217,728	268,435,455
29	268,435,456	536,870,911
30	536,870,912	

£10,737,418.23

Naturally, we assume you will be far too gracious a winner to insist on the bet actually being paid. If you do insist, and he can afford it, may he pay you in pennies.

AT THE END OF THE DAY

Death is a fact of life. Or is it a fact of death? Wittgenstein would have known. Or would he? God knows! Of course he does, which is the point of this trick.

The Effect
The magician tells the story of two men who, having reached the end of their days, died at exactly the same second, in the same minute, in the same hour, on the same day, in different places, and went to Heaven. As both men approached the Pearly Gates they saw St Peter idly trying to make a model aeroplane out of a piece of paper. It wasn't a busy day.

Both men sought admission. 'What sort of lives have you led?' asked St Peter.

The first man instantly replied that 50 per cent of his life had been blameless, while the other 50 per cent had been full of sin. Not big sins but lots of little forgivable ones that had mounted up.

The second man, who was basically honest, immediately confessed that half his life had been wasted in sinful pursuits, but the other half had followed a Christian path.

'I see,' said St Peter, scratching his beard. 'Well, this creates a problem, because there is only room for one inside. And I certainly can't choose between you.' There was a heavenly silence before St Peter spoke again. 'I have an idea which may solve the problem. Look, I'll fold this paper up like this and I'll cut it into two pieces like so. As you can see, the pieces in my left hand are slightly larger than the pieces in my right hand. You must decide between you who will receive what. Who gets these pieces?' He waved his right hand. 'And who gets these pieces?' He waved his left hand.

'Why?' asked the first man.

'Because one of them is a ticket to Heaven,' St Peter replied.

The first man looked at St Peter's left hand that held the larger pieces and reasoned that it would be wise not to appear to be greedy. And so, for the first time ever, he went for the smaller pieces, something he would never have done during his life. And he snatched them from St Peter's right hand. The second man was left with no choice but to take the larger pieces from St Peter's left hand.

Both men unfolded their paper. The first man assembled his pieces, laying them out to spell the word HELL, and that's where he went. Zap! In a puff of smoke. The second man's paper unfolded to reveal a large cross, which was his ticket to Heaven and salvation.

You see the first man had lied. His life was not equally good and bad. His tally was 49 per cent good and 51 per cent bad. Just 1 per cent difference. God knew that!

The Secret
All you need is a piece of A4 paper. Look at the diagrams and make the following folds:

1. A to B. Crease well. FIG. 1
2. C to D. Crease well. FIG. 2
3. E to F. Crease well. FIG. 3
4. F to G. Crease very well. FIG. 4
5. Cut vertically from H to I. FIG. 5
6. Push the two smaller, loose pieces in the left hand across, on top of the right-hand pieces, retaining the single large piece in the left hand.

Hold the larger pieces in your left hand, the smaller pieces in your right hand.

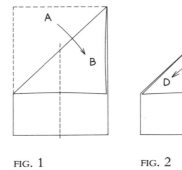

FIG. 1   FIG. 2

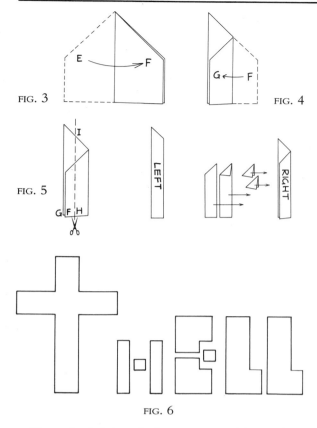

FIG. 3

FIG. 4

FIG. 5

FIG. 6

1. Multiply it by 2
2. Add 5
3. Multiply by 5
4. Multiply by 10
5. Add his age
6. Subtract 365
7. Add 115.

Finally the magician takes the calculator back, removes the paper strip and promptly announces the age and shoe size of his friend.

The Secret

If ever a trick justified the phrase 'self-working', this is it. Try it out by entering your own shoe size and age. When you receive the calculator back from your colleague, simply press the equals sign – discreetly. When you remove the paper strip the last two figures will be the age and the preceding figure or figures will be the shoe size.

'BEAT THE CALCULATOR'

This is a two-person challenge calculation trick in which the magician's mental abilities apparently function quicker than a calculator.

The Effect

The magician designates two spectators as assistants A and B. On a piece of paper he writes the letter A and, spaced away from it, he writes the letter B.

He asks spectator A to give him any three-figure number comprised of different digits. He writes this number down under both letter A and letter B.

He then asks spectator B for a three-figure number, which he writes down below the figures under letter A. He states he would like to contribute a number, which he writes down below the figure under letter B.

The conditions of the challenge are that both spectators have a calculator. Each will multiply the figures in their respective columns, then, working in tandem, will add their totals together to achieve a final sum. The magician will attempt to achieve the same result doing

Place the left-hand pieces to one side, unfold the right-hand pieces and lay out the word HELL. Then unfold the left-hand piece to reveal a cross. FIG. 6

Match your actions to suit the story and it's an interesting novelty for a tea-break.

CALCULATING MAGIC

When things get a little too hectic for comfort in the office, try a few of these stunts on your friends. A brief magical respite from the relentless demands of the day may lighten the load and will help you function better.

The Effect

The office magician gives a calculator to a friend. The display has been covered with a strip of paper taped to the calculator.

The magician instructs his friend to enter the size of his shoe. Then to:

the calculations mentally. Who will be quickest to complete the sum correctly? It goes without saying, but I'll say it anyway, that it's the magician, and by quite a margin!

The Secret

I'll teach you this by an example. You will have written the letters A and B, spaced out on your sheet of paper, and we'll assume the first spectator has given you number 631. So you write the number under both A and B:

A	B
631	631

The second assistant, spectator B, gives you the number 874, which you write under column A:

A	B
631	631
874	

You now say it's your turn to contribute a number, which is apparently random. In fact you mentally subtract the second number given, 874, from your secret key number 999. This gives 125, which you write in column B:

A	B
631	631
874	125

Alert each spectator to do the following sums on their calculators.

Spectator A will multiply the figures in his column:

$$\begin{array}{r} A \\ 631 \\ \times\ 874 \\ \hline \end{array}$$

Spectator B will multiply the figures in his column:

$$\begin{array}{r} B \\ 631 \\ \times\ 125 \\ \hline \end{array}$$

They will then add their totals together. The magician calls 'Go' to start.

Within seconds of calling 'Go' the magician has written the figure 630,369 in large letters on his piece of paper and slapped his pen down to indicate completion. Both spectators will still be fiddling with their calculators, which will eventually result in the following sums:

$$\begin{array}{cc} A & B \\ 631 & 631 \\ \times\ 874 & \times\ 125 \\ \hline 551{,}494 & +\quad 78{,}875\ =\ 630{,}369 \end{array}$$

The formula the magician applies is to subtract 1 from the top number of both columns, giving 630, which he instantly writes down. He then writes down the difference between 630 and 999, which is 369. So he has achieved the correct calculation incredibly quickly in comparison to the spectators using calculators.

In brief the formula is:

The magician's number is the difference between the second (spectator B's) number given and 999.
Subtract 1 from the top numbers and write it down, then the difference between this number and 999 and write it down.

Try it with different examples of your own and you will appreciate how quickly it can be done. For your presentation you may care to patter on about how, despite the advance of technology and computer science, there are some things the human brain can still do better, and then launch into the trick. Do it only once in front of the same group of people.

'CALCU-PUZZLES'

There is magic, sometimes, in the way you look at things. This little rhyme explains what the following is all about.

Here are the puzzles,
Here are the ways.
Where are the answers?
In the displays.

1. Greetings
   07734
2. Which company?
   $.39 \times .39 + .0039 - .00131 + 142 \times 5 =$
3. What every golfer doesn't want
   $1,956 \times 4 + 153 \times 4 =$
4. The Duchess of York flying a plane
   $.023 \times 3 + 10,141 \times 5 =$
5. Jayne Mansfield's assets
   $202 \times 41 + 5 \times 7 - .082 =$
6. In Charlie Chaplin's film *The Gold Rush* is a classic scene in which . . .
   $$
   \begin{aligned}
   17 \times 2 \quad &= \\
   + \; 57,074 \; &= \\
   - \; 56,594 \; &= \\
   + \; 2,531 \; &= \\
   \div \; 6,090 \; &= \\
   \times \; 1,028 \; &= \\
   + \; 3,191 \; &= \\
   - \; 3,654 \; &= \\
   + \; 34,956 \; &=
   \end{aligned}
   $$
7. Who played Rick in *Casablanca*?
   $2,572 + 87 \times 12 =$

'CALCALENDAR'

The first month of the last decade of the twentieth century sounds portentous enough to warrant teaching you some magic using the calendar. The addition of a calculator not only makes the effects incredibly easy to perform, but somehow adds a rather mysterious overtone of apparent difficulty to these intriguing mathematical stunts.

The Effect

A colleague selects any three horizontally consecutive dates in the month. He adds them together and tells you the total. You enter the figure into your magic calculator, perform one function and immediately tell him the selected dates.

The Secret

As an example, we'll say your colleague gave you a total of 27. Enter 27 and divide it by 3 – the result is 9 and will be the middle number of the three consecutive dates. Obviously the previous number is one less, 1 = 8, and the next number is + 1 = 10. So you immediately

announce the dates as the 8th, 9th and 10th.

This is a very basic example, which of course can be done mentally without using a calculator, but its use implies a difficult calculation, serving to divert attention from the simplicity of the method. An added touch would be to announce the days before the dates. For example, 'Twenty-seven. It must be a Monday, Tuesday or Wednesday. I think it's the 8th, 9th and 10th.'

1990		JANUARY			1990	
M	T	W	T	F	S	S
1	2	3	4	5	6	7
8	9	10	11	12	13	14
15	16	17	18	19	20	21
22	23	24	25	26	27	28
29	30	31				

This sounds better than it actually is, because, provided you know on what day the month starts, in our example the 1st, then the 8th, which is exactly one week later, must also fall on a Monday. As does the 15th, the 22nd and the 29th. If you look at the calendar for the year 1990 all you need to ask is what month he wants. If he says April, a quick glance tells you it begins on a Sunday, so the next four weeks, the 8th, 15th, 22nd and 29th (all additions of 7), will fall on a Sunday, as the 4th, 11th, 18th and 25th are all Wednesdays, and so on.

Here's another example using January again. Your colleague selects three consecutive dates on a horizontal, adds them together and gives you the total of 72. Enter it in your calculator and divide it by 3, which gives you 24. So 24 minus 1 = 23. And 24 + 1 = 25. The dates are the 23rd, 24th and 25th.

But also you subtract 21 (which is three weeks: 3×7) from 23, leaving 2 a Tuesday, as you know that the 1st of the month falls on a Monday. So you announce the days, then the dates, or both together as 'Monday, the 23rd, Tuesday, the 24th and Wednesday, the 25th.'

A little practice will prove how simple this is, and it will puzzle those who know the basic effect.

A variation is to have somebody total three figures vertically. For example they give you a figure of 39, which you divide by 3, giving you the middle number of 13. From which you subtract 7, leaving 6 the first date, and, by adding 7, making 20 the third date. So the three selected dates are the 6th, 13th and 20th, all Saturdays.

1990　　**JANUARY**　　**1990**

M	T	W	T	F	S	S
1	2	3	4	5	6	7
8	9	10	11	12	13	14
15	16	17	18	19	20	21
22	23	24	25	26	27	28
29	30	31				

For a more ambitious presentation here are the formulas for groups of four, five, six and seven consecutive horizontal dates.

Four:
Divide the given total by four to get four consecutive dates. If there is a remainder ignore it. The resulting figure will be the second date of the four consecutive dates. So the other three are easy to work out.

Five:
Dividing the given total by 5 tells you the date number in third position. Again, it's easy to work out the other dates.

Six:
Divide the given total by 6 and, ignoring any remainder, the result will be the third of the six consecutive dates, so it's easy to work out the other dates.

Seven:
Dividing the given total by 7 will give you the fourth date in the row of seven, and it's easy to work out the others.

You could perform all of these at once as a multiple presentation. Start by doing a three-date version to serve as an example. Then assign four, five, six and seven dates to each of the four spectators. You can dress this up a little by assigning each a different calendar month to choose from and divert them further from the mechanics of the trick. If you've really done your homework on the calendar and can name the days each date falls on, you will have a very powerful effect indeed. The key to the presentation is speed. The quicker you seem to make the calculations, the more impressive the feat

becomes. And if, once you're familiar with it, you can forgo using the calculator, you'll have a reputation-maker.

If you want to do a similar thing with a series of vertical dates here are the formulas you'll need to determine four and five dates. And there can't be more than five, can there?

Four:
Subtract 42 from the given total, then divide by 4. The result will be the first date in the series of four. To find the second, simply add 7, add another 7 for the third date and another 7 for the fourth date.

Five:
Subtract 70 from the given total, then divide by 5. The result will be the first date in the series of five. The addition of 7 will tell you the second date. Further additions of 7 will reveal the third, fourth and fifth dates.

We can take these principles a stage further to demonstrate a couple of strong tricks on the same theme.

The Effect

A spectator, unseen by you, encircles a block of any nine dates in any month on the calendar. As an example we'll say he chooses the following dates:

11th	12th	13th
18th	19th	20th
25th	26th	27th

1990　　**JANUARY**　　**1990**

M	T	W	T	F	S	S
1	2	3	4	5	6	7
8	9	10	11	12	13	14
15	16	17	18	19	20	21
22	23	24	25	26	27	28
29	30	31				

Ask him to give you the total of any two diagonally opposite dates, so he totals either 11 and 27 or 13 and 25. Both add up to 38. If you divide this total by 2, it gives 19, the centre date in the block of nine. This makes it easy to determine the dates on either side of it in the same row, and by subtracting 7 the dates in the row above, and by adding 7 the ones in the row below.

A good alternative is to ask him to name the lowest date in his block of nine. When he does so, you instruct him to add all nine dates together and give you the total. Before he even begins, you are able to tell him the total: 171.

The formula for this is to add 8 to his lowest date, which he tells you is 11. This gives 19, which you multiply by 9, giving 171.

A few trial runs will convince you of the practicality of these methods, but you'll only gauge their effectiveness by performing them.

THE KNIGHT'S TOUR

We could best categorize this astonishing feat as cerebral or mental magic. As a demonstration of your remarkable mental agility it can hardly be bettered. Although it utilizes the chess knight and the chessboard layout, its appeal is not limited only to those with an understanding of the game. The presentation is simple and direct enough to be followed by any observer. This fact was confirmed by Professor Hoffman in 1895 in his book *Puzzles Old and New*, when he wrote, 'But there is one particular chess puzzle, the so-called Knight's Tour, which requires no knowledge of chess, and may be attempted with success even by a person quite unacquainted with the game.' Hoffman added a footnote later in the book. 'The Knight's Tour is frequently performed as a show feat, by means of a mnemonic formula.'

The Tour certainly became a staple of various memory courses for sale to the general public, where it was treated as a useful exercise to practise mnemonic systems.

As a performance piece, it was traced by Cyril Shields in his book *Broadcast Conjuring Tricks*, published in 1930, to a demonstration by a Hungarian, Baron Von Kempelen, in Germany in the year 1770. Shields referred to this as the earliest record of the trick he could find. What is not made clear by this is whether the Baron actually presented the tour as a trick or as a mnemonic demonstration. The difference between the two is that as a magic trick you commit nothing to memory and resort to a secret method; whereas the other is a feat of genuine memory or the application of a memory system.

Many famous magicians have included the Knight's Tour in their repertoire, because they well knew the impact it had on audiences, who credited the performer with remarkable mental powers. For a minimum of effort it will do the same for you. Ironically, the trick is particularly baffling to chess players.

The Effect

The magician exhibits a piece of paper on which is drawn a chessboard with every square numbered in sequence from 1 to 64. He gives it, along with a pen, to a spectator. Next the magician is blindfolded and positioned to sit facing away from his audience. He explains that, of all the chess pieces, the knight moves from square to square in the most unusual way. It can move in any one of four directions at a time; for example: one square forward and two squares to either left or right; alternatively, two squares forward and one square either left or right. Either of these choices can also be made going sideways or backwards on the board. He states that he will attempt to move the knight over every square of the chessboard without touching the same square twice. Not only that, he will start the Knight's Tour from any square on the board the assisting spectator chooses.

The spectator calls out number 8 as the starting-point.

'Very well,' says the magician. 'Put the point of your pen on the eighth square and keep it on the paper, because you are now going to draw a continuous line to chart the progress of the knight on his tour of the board. Now draw a line from number 8 to 14, then continue to 24, then on to 7, then 22, then 5, on to 15, progress to 32, then to 47, now go to . . .'

And so the blindfolded magician continues the Knight's Tour until eventually the spectator's pen will reach square 8 again. The magician has achieved exactly what he said he would, and demonstrated amazing mental powers in the process, either as a remarkably skilful chess-player or a man with a phenomenal memory.

All that remains is for him to remove the blindfold and take his applause at the successful

1	2	3	4	5	6	7	8
9	10	11	12	13	14	15	16
17	18	19	20	21	22	23	24
25	26	27	28	29	30	31	32
33	34	35	36	37	38	39	40
41	42	43	44	45	46	47	48
49	50	51	52	53	54	55	56
57	58	59	60	61	62	63	64

point, find it; then call the next number, 61, after that 55, followed by 40, then 23, 8, 14, etc.

Of course you don't just reel off the numbers as though you were reading a list. You introduce pauses whilst you think, brief moments of indecision, hesitations and surges of confidence when you rattle off a series of numbers, building to the completion of the effect. Leave the completed tour with the spectator as a souvenir.

If this becomes a favourite of yours, and you have occasion to perform it for people who

1

conclusion of his demonstration of the tour.

The Secret

The only real skill involved in the trick is in the presentation, emphasizing the difficulty of the feat and varying the pace of the demonstration to sustain and build interest as the trick reaches its climax.

The physical properties required include a piece of card small enough to palm in your hand, on which you have written the following sequence of numbers.

have seen you present it before, there is a small possibility that a friend, especially a chess-playing friend, might realize you are using the same sequence of numbers, even though the starting-points will be different. So, as an option, here is a different sequence of moves that achieve the same effect.

1	60	37	53	23	32	62	49
11	45	20	43	8	47	52	34
21	39	26	33	14	64	58	17
4	29	36	27	24	54	41	2
10	12	30	44	7	48	51	19
25	6	13	61	22	63	57	9
35	16	28	55	5	46	42	3
50	31	38	40	15	56	59	18

1	48	10	51	46	37	58	32
11	63	4	57	29	22	41	47
17	53	14	42	35	7	26	64
2	59	8	27	45	24	9	54
12	49	23	44	30	39	3	60
6	34	40	38	13	56	20	50
16	19	55	21	28	62	5	33
31	25	61	36	43	52	15	18

Secondly, you require a blindfold, which, as well as enhancing the presentation, allows you to peer down along the line of your nose to read the numbers on the card hidden in your hand **1**. Because that's all you do, whatever number is called as the starting-point. Our example was 8, so you just read the next number, moving vertically down each column, then to the top of the next column. If 44 is called as the starting-

You could prepare sheets of paper for the demonstration, personalized with your name or your company's name and relevant slogans. The tour would make for a formidable demonstration piece for a sales presentation. The only thing that limits its possibilities for use in your private or working life is your imagination. And by the end of this book a magical imagination should be within your compass. To further stimulate that imagination, consider this idea applied to a sales presentation.

As you know the sequence of moves prior to performance, you could write one, two or three letters of the alphabet in each numbered square. To the onlooker it would look like a totally random grouping of letters. But at the end of the Knight's Tour presentation you could follow exactly the knight's numerical tour with an alphabetical one that spells out a message. Here's an example of how it works.

If you wanted a sentence to read 'Do you believe in magic?' you would break up the sentence in the following way. In square 8 you write D. In square 14 – OY, in square 24 – OU, and so on. The letters in the sentence will be allocated like this: 8 – D, 14 – OY, 24 – OU, 7 – B, 22 – EL, 5 – IE, 15 – VE, 32 – I, 47 – N, 64 – M, 54 – AG, 48 – I, 63 – C.

To demonstrate the message you follow the numerical tour and write down the letters in the progressive sequence DOYOUBELIEVEIN-MAGIC. To point up the sense for those who don't recognise it, strike a line between each word: DO/YOU/BELIEVE/IN/MAGIC.

For sales presentations, a large square on a blackboard is perfect for people viewing from a distance. To achieve an effective message, all you have to work out is something appropriate to fill sixty-four squares, whether it's a serious company message, or a tasteful limerick for a group of highly motivated salesmen or a novel resignation.

On a personal level you might consider an unusual proposal of marriage to a chess-playing girl-friend, even an unusual greeting to be included in your income tax return. It's all down to your imagination. All you have to do is think magic.

IT'S NOT AS EASY AS YOU THINK

Once enormously popular as an advertising give away, particularly in America, this ingenious puzzle has all but disappeared from the magic scene. Its revival is long overdue. Perhaps this book will be the catalyst for its rediscovery. Its invention is credited to the American puzzle genius Sam Loyd.

The Effect
A pencil with a loop of string attached to one end is threaded through a buttonhole of a spectator's jacket, whilst he looks away **1**. He is then invited to remove the pencil from his

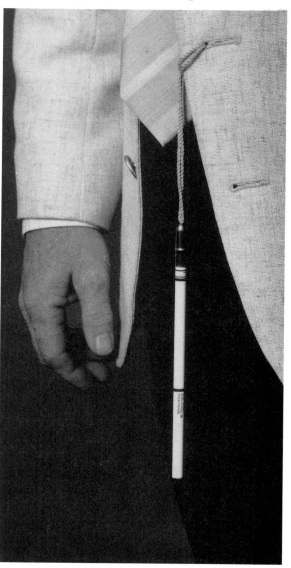

1

buttonhole. It seems easy enough until he tries, when he quickly realises he can't do it. The loop of string isn't long enough to go over the end of the pencil **2**, therefore it can't be

2

Pull the buttonhole through the loop of string, pulling sufficient material through it to enable you to push the point of the pencil through the buttonhole **4**, then pull the pencil completely through and slip the string loop off

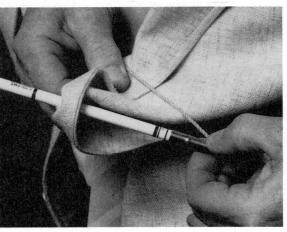

4

released **3**. But you, the magician, can get it off as easily as you got it on.

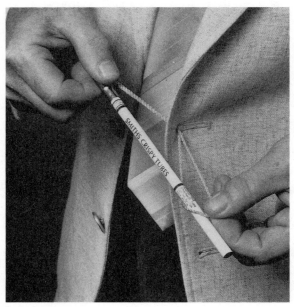

3
The Secret
It should be obvious to you, if you study the photographs, that the way you get it on is also the way you get it off.

the cloth so the pencil dangles from the buttonhole as in the first photograph.

To remove the pencil, simply reverse the moves. Pull sufficient cloth of the jacket through the loop to allow you to push the loop end of the pencil through the buttonhole, pull it completely through and away from the jacket and the loop will come with it. Straighten the jacket and leave the spectator mystified – unless you choose to show him how to do it. We hope you won't. To make one up, all you need is some string, a small elastic band and a modicum of ingenuity.

'JUST ONE OF THE MIRACLES WE DO'

One subject of ongoing debate amongst creators of magic is the degree of impossibility that an effect should present. If a trick is so amazing and altogether inexplicable that the spectating audience hasn't a ghost of a chance of even attempting an explanation, then, it is argued, that trick is self-defeating, because its intrinsic impossibility allows the audience to dismiss it too readily as a con. To vanish the Eiffel Tower and bring it back defies magical belief, because it is too implausible to be credible. Another viewpoint would argue that it really is a question of scale and location. If you vanish a foot-high model of the Eiffel Tower from under a tea-towel on the kitchen table, then you have a great trick that is magically credible to the spectator and will therefore genuinely engage his interest.

Here is a trick which to the spectator is totally impossible, yet its scale and setting offset its being too easily dismissed. In the context of its performance this is a reputation-maker.

The Effect

Let us imagine that you are meeting someone and your objective is to persuade him of the benefits your company's expertise can bring to his business. Here's how a little magic can provide an unusual approach to impressing a prospective client.

Having been made welcome, Mr X is seated with coffee in hand. 'Do you believe in magic?' you ask. This is probably the last thing Mr X was expecting to hear. Whatever his reply, continue, 'Before we get down to business, I'd like you to help me with a little experiment. Here is a pack of cards. Examine them and, when you are happy that they are just a normal pack, give them a thorough shuffle. OK, now I want you to select a card but in such a way that neither of us can possibly know what it is. I'll hold them face down and I'll cover them with this handkerchief. Now what I would like you to do with your left hand is to feel the cards through the handkerchief and cut them. Hold them above the pack and with your right hand reach under the handkerchief and take the card that you cut at. Got it? Good. Then put it face down on the desk and keep your hand flat on top of it. Now replace the cards you cut. I'll take away the handkerchief and will put the cards down here.

'So you have a selected card under your hand which, I think you will agree, neither of us can possibly know the value of. Now from this point on I am going to say absolutely nothing other than ask you to call my secretary on the intercom. I'll put a pen and paper here for her to use, but from now on I'll remain silent.'

Mr X buzzes through for your secretary. She enters, approaches the desk, picks up the pen

and paper and writes something. She tears one sheet of paper from the pad and places it face down on the desk next to Mr X's hand, which is covering his selected card. She then leaves the room. Mr X turns the paper over. On it is written, 'You have selected the five of diamonds.' He reveals his selected card. It is indeed the five of diamonds.

The Secret

A combination of techniques makes the effect possible. The first is a subtle glimpse and force of a card. The second silently cues the value of the forced card to a confederate using a prearranged code. Both techniques are quite easy to learn with a little genuine practice.

The props you need for the trick are a felt-tip pen with a cap, a ballpoint pen with a cap, a press-in ballpoint pen with no cap, a large opaque handkerchief or scarf and a notepad from which single sheets can be easily torn.

I'll start by teaching the code that you and your secretary will need to learn. The value of any chosen card is directly conveyed by:

1. The choice of pen used
2. The condition and position of the pen
3. The relation of the pen to the notepad. Even number cards will always have the pen on the notepad; odd ones next to the notepad.

Study the following with the appropriate pen in hand and you will see how straightforward the card code is. To avoid any confusion, when the pen is described as having its cap on, it means on the pen covering its writing point.

Felt-tip pen (cards A, 2, 3, 4, 5, 6)
Odd cards (pen only next to notepad)

Ace – pen with cap on
Three – pen with cap off
Five – pen with cap on non-writing end of pen

Even cards (with pen on notepad)

2 ♣   4 ♦   6 ♠

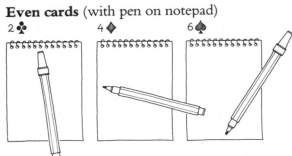

Two – pen with cap on and on notepad
Four – pen with cap off and on notepad
Six – pen with cap on non-writing end of pen and on notepad

Ballpoint pen with cap (cards 7, 8, 9, 10)
Odd cards (pen only)

Seven – ballpoint with cap on
Nine – ballpoint with cap off

Even cards   8 ♣   10 ♠

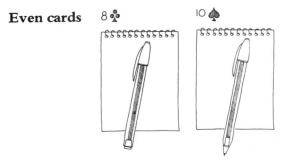

Eight – ballpoint with cap on and on notepad
Ten – ballpoint with cap on non-writing end of pen and on notepad

Press-in ballpoint (the court cards J, Q, K)

Jack – ballpoint top end not pressed in
Queen – ballpoint end pressed in and on notepad
King – ballpoint pressed in.

Summary

Felt-tip with cap – ace to six
Ballpoint with cap – seven to 10
Press-in ballpoint – jack, queen, king
All odd cards – pen only
All even cards – pen and notepad
For the two pens that have caps there are three conditions:
1. Pen with cap on
2. Pen with cap off
3. Pen with cap on non-writing end of pen.

The card suits are coded by using the word 'CHaSeD' as a mnemonic. Look at it again, the capitals stand for clubs, hearts, spades and diamonds. Imagine a clock-face with clubs at twelve o'clock, hearts at three o'clock, spades at six o'clock and diamonds at nine o'clock. No matter which pen is used, when you place it on your desk for your secretary's use, simply point the writing end of the pen to the appropriate hour from her viewpoint. Clubs/ twelve o'clock will be furthest away from her, spades/six o'clock nearest to her.

Let's run through the trick with the props. Mr X is shuffling the pack thoroughly. You need to glimpse the bottom card of the pack. As Mr X is in the process of tidying and squaring up the pack and handing it to you, you may be able to glimpse the bottom card. In the circumstances it's perfectly natural for you to be looking at him and at the cards. So the opportunity may present itself naturally. If, however, he's a card-player and shuffles and squares neatly without exposing or flashing the face of the bottom card, here's what you do. Take the pack and hold it in your left hand in the following way. First hold the pack with your left thumb across the back of the top card and all four fingers against the right long edge. Now with your right hand move the pack back and a little deeper into your left hand. Curl your left forefinger over the top short edge of the pack so that it can easily touch the tip of your left thumb. This is called the Mechanic's Grip.

With the pack held in this grip, you will find it easy to unfold a handkerchief and hold it up by the corners using the thumbs and forefingers of both hands. In the process of doing so you can glimpse the bottom card of the pack in a very subtle way. Hold the pack in your left hand in the Mechanic's Grip position, with the back of your left hand resting on the table. Now turn your hand over so that the thumb and fingertips are touching the table. Look at the face card of the pack between your first and second fingers. You will clearly see the indice of the card but also notice that your second finger covers the indice from the viewpoint of Mr X sitting opposite you. Don't stare at the exposed indice, a casual glance will be sufficient to see and remember the card as you busy yourself with the handkerchief. For our example we'll use the five of clubs.

Continue by explaining that you are going to have him select a card in such a way that neither of you will know what it is. Cover your hand holding the cards with the handkerchief and explain that he will cut a portion of cards through the handkerchief with one hand, reach under it with the other hand and take the top card from the lower portion. This selected card he places face down on the table and covers with his free hand. He then replaces the cards he cut, through the handkerchief, on to the lower portion you are still holding. You take away the handkerchief and put the cards aside on the desk. Nothing has happened to excite his suspicion. In fact you have forced the five of clubs on him in the following way. When you cover the cards with the handkerchief **1** in the

2 (exposed view)

process of feeling the pack through the cloth with your right hand, separate the bottom card slightly from the rest of the pack with your left thumb and fingers **2**. As you demonstrate cutting and lifting half of the covered pack, actually lift the entire pack but retain the bottom card, the five of clubs, in your left hand. As you are telling him that he will reach under and take the card he cut at, curl your left forefinger under the five of clubs and turn it over. Then put the pack back into your left hand, which you describe for his benefit as replacing the top cut-off portion.

The condition of the pack is face down on top of a face-up five of clubs. This sets you up for the force. Get him to lift off a portion of the cards but only high enough to keep your left hand covered. As he cuts the cards curl your left forefingers under the remainder of the pack and turn it over. When he reaches under the handkerchief with his free hand he will take the five of clubs **3**. As soon as his hand has taken

1

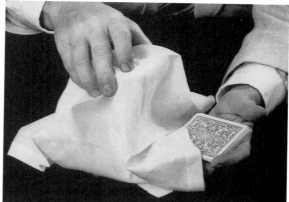

3 (exposed view)

the card and as he is putting it on the table, turn the cards in your left hand over again. Now have him replace the cut-off portion of cards and place them and the handkerchief aside.

All that remains for you to do is cue the card to your secretary. Pick up a felt-tip pen, take off the cap and put it on the non-writing end, then place it next to a notepad with the tip pointing at twelve o'clock from her viewpoint. The trick is done. Proceed as described, and you will amaze Mr X. His response might even amaze you.

Although this has taken some describing it is all really quite simple. Practice is made marvellously easy in working conditions at the office. Lay out the appropriate pen in cue position, on or next to a notepad and simply vary it every time your secretary enters your room. Within a very short period of time the code will be second nature to you both. You can of course work this at home with your wife or girl friend. Obviously the trick is not confined to the workplace.

One final touch of finesse is to have a known card, for example, the queen of hearts, on the bottom of the pack prior to shuffling. If you spot it's still there after the pack has been shuffled you can work the following variation. Have the message 'Magic Marketing [substitute your company name] predict you will select the queen of hearts' typed on to a piece of paper and sealed in an envelope prior to performance. Force the queen of hearts. Ask Mr X to call your secretary. She enters with the envelope and hands it to him and leaves without saying a word. He should be suitably impressed when he opens the envelope and turns over his chosen card.

How's it done? Your secretary always carries the envelope when you perform this trick. If you haven't laid out a pen and paper for her to write on, she will know the queen of hearts is the selected card. Doing nothing actually cues the card. If, however, the pen and notepad are laid out ready to use, she simply follows the usual procedure and never offers the envelope. It's perfectly normal for a secretary to be holding an envelope. She can also be carrying her own pen and notepad to use, ignoring the ones you have so considerately laid out for her. She only needs to look at them to know the chosen card. The reason for using a notepad and not a single sheet of paper is so she can write standing up. If she wrote on a single sheet on the desk, Mr X would be able to see it and you would forfeit the element of surprise.

You may like to think of other ways of coding the selected cards. To further stimulate you here are two suggestions. If you used three different pens and one pencil you could code the suit of the card using the CHaSeD mnemonic in the following way:

Clubs – a press-in ballpoint
Hearts – a see-through, clear-body ballpoint
Spades – a fountain pen
Diamonds – a pencil.

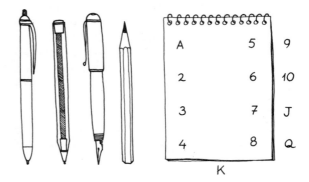

To cue the value of the card look at the diagram. Card values 1 to 8 are cued by imagining the notepad as being quartered in four horizontal strips. Simply put the point of the appropriate pen or pencil on the imaginary coded value. For nine through to the king put the point of the pen on the imaginary coded value next to the notepad. This is a very effective variation, which can be practised every time your secretary enters the room. Placing the pen or pencil on or next to the notepad is so normal and casual it will go unnoticed.

An even simpler variation is for you to shuffle the cards, keeping the same card on the bottom each time, and to force that particular card. Then there is very little to rehearse. Although it lacks the impossible conditions in the way the trick is set up in the first two versions it may be just as effective. That's for you to decide.

CHAPTER 5
MAGIC OUT TO LUNCH

To be able to fill leisure intelligently is the last product of civilization. – *Arnold Toynbee*

It's amazing how many props there are on a dining-table just waiting to be picked up and magished with by you. If you can do magic in the office, then it's a racing certainty they'll expect you to do something over lunch. And you'll not disappoint them, even though it all appears so impromptu, using as props every-day objects. And that's the secret: the essence of a good magician is his ability to perform any time, anywhere.

RUBBER SPOON

A nice old visual gag is making a pencil appear to go soft and bendy. Hold a pencil, about 3 cm (1½ in) from one end, between your first finger and thumb horizontal in relation to the table **1**.

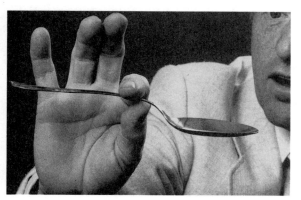

1

Move your hand up and down in small, quick, rhythmic movements. Keep doing this and gradually lessen the tension of your grip on the pencil. Watch the pencil carefully as you do this until the pencil looks like it is made of rubber.

Once you see the visual effect as you do it, you'll understand 'the feel' that is necessary to make it work. Now try it with a spoon.

The shape of a spoon actually enhances the visual effect. The illusion of a rubber spoon is perfect. Practise in front of a mirror holding the spoon half-way along the handle.

To present this trick at the dinner-table, pick up a spoon and tap the bowl on the table a couple of times. Then pull the spoon between your hands as though stretching it. Perform the rubber spoon effect a few times, then hold the spoon at each end and pretend to compress it by pushing inward. Tap the spoon on the table a couple of times and take a bow.

SPOON BENDER

Long before Uri Geller made his name inter-nationally famous, magicians were bending spoons as a little gag.

Clip the stem of a tablespoon, where it meets the bowl, at the base of your right third and fourth fingers. Curl your fingers around the stem and press the ball of your thumb against the underside of the end of the stem. Place the fingers of your left hand on top of your right fingers and press your left thumb against the nail of your right thumb. Put the underside, that is, convex side of the bowl, on the table. This position affords the leverage to bend the handle of the spoon by pushing the end of the stem up with your thumb **1**.

What you actually do is allow your thumbs to slip over the end of the spoon and pretend to bend the spoon. The stem is hidden behind your fingers as you simulate slowly bending it. Then lift the 'bent' spoon and drop it on the table. The spectators will be surprised to see the spoon isn't distorted at all.

An improvement – credited to Derek

Vernon, Dai Vernon's son, and Slydini – is the subtle use of a small silver coin **2**. This is held

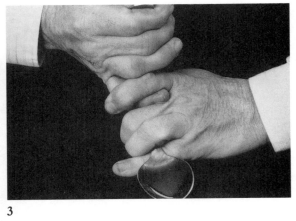

3

1

2

4 (exposed view)

very good friends or use your own cutlery.

An item of esoteric information, courtesy of Martin Gardner, is that drinking a glass of water whilst keeping the bowl of a spoon in your mouth cures hiccups. Can this really be the solution the world has been waiting for? Try it and see.

against the top end of the spoon by the right forefingers so that only the slightest curve of the coin is visible. Proceed exactly as described, but hold the coin in the same position the end of the spoon would be as you bent it **3** and **4**. The illusion is perfect. Drop the spoon on the table, retaining the coin hidden in your hand and pocketing it at the first opportunity.

A lovely gag to play on those who will have seen you perform this before is actually to bend the spoon and drop it on the table. You'll get a good surprise laugh. But make sure they are

THINK TAP

Here's a chance for you to go mental during or after lunch and baffle your friends at the same time.

The Effect

The magician arranges seven objects on the table. A friend is asked to think of one of them. The magician then taps each of them in turn with a fork. For each tap, the friend has to mentally spell out one letter of the name of the object he has in mind. On the last letter spelt he should stop. Amazingly, the magician's fork will be on the same object thought of by the friend.

The Secret

The trick is infallible, provided you exercise your judgement and your memory – your judgement in choosing a friend who can spell and your memory in committing the following seven numbers and articles to memory.

1. Cup
2. Salt
3. Glass
4. Napkin
5. Ashtray
6. Matchbox
7. Cigarette

Once your friend has an object in mind, and you have told him what to do, deliberately and slowly tap the seven objects in the following sequence, having first isolated them in a random order on the table **1**.

1

First tap	–	any object
Second tap	–	any object
Third tap	–	No. 1 Cup
Fourth tap	–	No. 2 Salt
Fifth tap	–	No. 3 Glass
Sixth tap	–	No. 4 Napkin
Seventh tap	–	No. 5 Ashtray
Eighth tap	–	No. 6 Matchbox
Ninth tap	–	No. 7 Cigarette

The trick works itself and will stand one or two repetitions, which will be enough to fool your lunch-mates.

RUBBER DOUGH

Good timing is crucial in the performance of magic. Here's a fun item for the dining-table which, properly performed, is very surprising to spectators.

The Effect

The magician, who is seated at a table in a restaurant, takes a roll from the bread-basket. 'I wonder if these are made with the new rubber dough everyone's talking about,' he muses.

This should provoke a quizzical response. 'Yes, apparently they have twice as much yeast as ordinary bread rolls,' he states. He throws the bread roll to the floor and it bounces back just like a rubber ball. The magician catches it, throws it down again and catches it as it bounces back up. 'That definitely is rubber dough,' he says as he breaks the roll in two and reaches for the butter.

The Secret

Hold the bread roll as though you were going to throw it to the floor so it would bounce back up for you to catch. That is what you are going to simulate doing **1**.

In slow motion this is what actually happens.

1

1. Throw the roll to the floor but don't release it. The throwing motion will carry your hand below the edge of the table and out of sight **2**. Keep the heel of your shoe on the floor but raise the sole from the floor.

2

2. At the moment the throwing movement stops, when ordinarily you release your grip on the bread roll, stamp your sole on the floor. If the floor is thickly carpeted, you may have to lift your entire foot and stamp. But do it with a minimum of body movement.

3. As soon as you hear the sound of your foot stamp, flip the roll straight up into

3

the air with a sharp wrist action, but not a bending action of the elbow. Make sure they don't see your hand come up with the throw **3**.

Count the entire action as three beats. Throw, stamp, flip up. Each action is counted on the beat. Try it in front of a mirror. Properly performed, it's very deceptive to both the eye and the ear.

BETTER THAN A FORTUNE COOKIE

One of the secrets of entertaining with magic in everyday situations is to use everyday articles that are obviously free from suspicion. Here's a good example.

The Effect
The magician picks up a bread roll and asks his lunch partner if they know what a fortune cookie is. Whatever the reply, he breaks the bread roll in two halves and there, sticking out of the centre of one half, is a coin. He picks it out, taps the crumbs off it and pockets it, saying, 'This is better than a fortune cookie. It's a fortune bread roll.'

The Secret
Hold a large coin in the curled fingers of your right hand between the first joints of your second and third fingers and the base of the

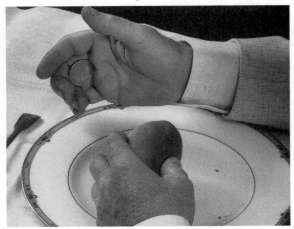

1

fingers. This is called the finger palm. It's a very natural palm which allows you to rest your hand casually on the table **1**.

Pick up a bread roll and break it in two in the following way. Hold it with your fingers under the roll and your thumbs on top. Push down with your thumbs as you pull up with your fingers, sufficient to break the crust only on the

2

bottom of the roll **2**. With your right fingers push the coin into the roll and angle it back into the centre of the right half of the roll **3**. Now

3

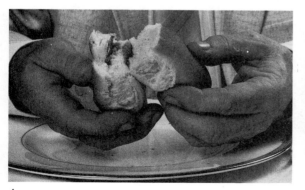

4

reverse the pressure, and by pushing up and out with your fingers break the roll and separate the halves. The coin will be sticking out of the half-roll in your right hand **4**.

Although these actions sound relatively simple, the effect requires practice so that you can perform it effortlessly. Although we wouldn't regard this as pure sleight of hand, it does require neat handling. Try practising in front of a mirror to achieve the desired effect.

I'LL BE DAMNED

When you read the description of the effect of this trick, you'll be impressed. Then, when you read the secret of the trick, you won't believe it possible. Having acquired the props to do the trick, when you try it out, you'll be amazed. This might just be the best trick in the book.

The Effect

After fiddling around for a while below the edge of the table, the magician eventually produces an empty drinking glass, to the mouth of which he has secured a piece of rubber sheet with an elastic band. The glass is completely sealed. On top of the rubber sheet are a tenpence piece and a penny **1**.

1

After standing the glass on the table he asks a spectator to select one of the coins. The tenpence piece is chosen. The magician then says, 'Look very closely. There's nothing in my hands, nothing up my sleeves, nothing in my head and nothing in the glass. Or is there?'

He presses lightly on the tenpence piece **2** and it visibly penetrates the rubber and drops into

2

3

the glass. The magician picks up the glass, takes the penny coin and rattles the glass. The tenpence piece is unmistakably inside the glass **3**.

The Secret

From a dental supply house you will need to purchase a small sheet of dental rubber dam. A thin grade of thickness will be ideal. Cut a 13cm (5 in) square piece from the sheet. Now with a tenpence coin balanced on the second and third fingertips of your right hand, place the rubber dam over the coin. Stretch the rubber between your hands as far as you can and push the coin up hard against the centre of the rubber. Keeping the coin in place, gradually release the tension on the stretched rubber **4**. As you do so you will feel the rubber grip the coin, to the extent that you can safely take your fingertips away. The rubber will not only keep the coin securely held but the rubber will now be so transparent that the coin actually appears to be on the rubber, instead of underneath it **5**,

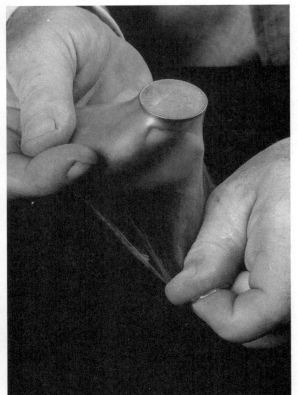

4

if you look from above. You can also use a pen to balance the coin when you stretch the rubber dam, if you like **6** and **7**.

Gently stretch the rubber sheet over the mouth of a glass and secure it around the edges with a rubber band. Place a penny coin on top of the sheet. The visual effect of two coins on top of a piece of rubber stretched over a glass is perfect. You simply can't tell that the tenpence coin is actually underneath.

To perform the trick, ask a spectator to choose one of the coins. If he says the penny, pick it up, give it to him and say, 'OK, that's your choice. I'll do the magic with this one.'

If he chooses the tenpence coin, proceed as described. The piece of rubber can be used many times before it will need replacing. The cost of purchasing the rubber dam will be one of the best magical investments you will ever make.

As this is an adult book, I feel I can also recommend a fine-grade prophylactic as an alternative to dental rubber dam.

5

6

7

CHAPTER 6
MAGIC AFTER HOURS

The main obligation is to amuse yourself
– *S.J. Perelman*

Magic is a wonderfully interactive hobby, tailor-made for the social mêlée of the modern bar. You can score real Brownie points here. Friendships and contacts are established, sometimes for life. But most important of all is the opportunity for you to have some fun and refine your magic skills into the bargain.

IF YOU CATCH IT, IT'S YOURS

Here are two fantastic bar stunts, one version of which Paul has performed to great effect on his BBC television series. This can be presented as a reaction test or even as a magic test of fitness to drive.

The Effect
The magician holds a banknote by one end in a vertical position. The spectator positions his fingers and thumb either side of the note without actually touching it **1**. The magician tells him that when you release the note he has to catch it. If he does so before it hits the floor, he can keep it. The spectator will fancy his chances, but in fact he has no chance. He can try a number of times, but he will never catch it. Your money is safe, but you can bank on it creating a lot of laughter.

The Secret
The reason you're on safe ground with this stunt is that, provided they follow your instructions, it really is impossible for them to catch it. The reason is physiological. By the time the message that the note has been released is received by the brain – which responds with the instruction to the fingers to catch it – it's too late. All this happens in milliseconds.

A couple of things to be aware of are that the

1

spectator is not allowed to drop his arm in order to catch the note nearer to the floor. And he must not anticipate the release of the note. He must react to it.

Paul has a super variation of this, using a pencil, which the magician holds horizontal to

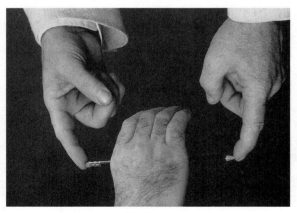

2

the floor between his index fingertips. The spectator holds his hand over the middle of the pencil in a 'ready to grab it' position **2**. The magician releases the pencil by moving his fingertips slightly apart at the same time, so that it remains horizontal as it drops.

The net result is the same: the spectator can't catch the pencil. Paul does this a few times, then lets the spectator hold the pencil while he attempts to grab it.

Naturally enough, he does catch it, every time. That's because there is a secret method to catching the pencil. But Paul has suggested that you may care to figure it out for yourself. This will provoke you into 'thinking like a magician' in order to solve the problem, which is one of the objectives of the book.

FANCY THAT!

The author has had a lot of fun with this quickie over the years. It's a sure fire ice-breaker, provided you judge the personality of your assistant correctly.

The Effect

The magician gets a male spectator to put his hand in an upright position on the table **1**. His

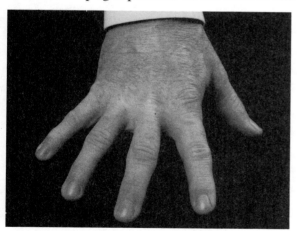

1

fingers are extended and open. The magician asks the spectator to bend his middle finger back so that the second knuckle is pressed on the table **2**.

'Now,' says the magician, 'I'm going to ask

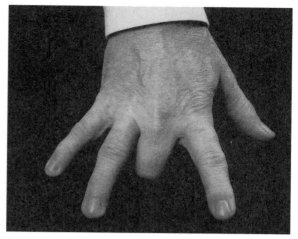

2

you three questions. Each question will be addressed to a different finger or thumb. If the answer is yes, you waggle the finger. If the answer is no, you don't move it. You understand that? OK. The first question is to your little finger. Do you like girls?'

The spectator waggles his little finger.

'He likes girls,' the magician says to the other spectators. 'The next question is to your thumb. Do you like kissing girls?'

The spectator waggles his thumb.

'He likes kissing girls,' the magician announces. 'And the last question is to your ring finger. Are you any good at kissing girls?'

The spectator will be unable to waggle his ring finger. The magician leaps in with 'You're no good at kissing girls! Fancy that, what an admission. Not many people would own up to that.' By now everybody will be laughing.

I've given you the basic patter line, but you may care to introduce your own variations, the suitability of which is dependent on the company you're in. Use your own good judgement.

The Secret

The reason they can't waggle their ring or third finger is that it is actually physically impossible to do so when the second finger is bent in as described.

One tip when performing this trick is to point to the finger or thumb you are addressing your question to, as some people can't follow instructions very well and get easily confused.

JUGGLE

Clowns and comedy jugglers have got a lot of mileage out of this classic stunt over the years. It's a big laugh-getter that will, in showbiz parlance, knock 'em dead.

The Effect

Standing at the bar, you tell your friends that you have been practising the most difficult feat of juggling in the world, and that you are proud to announce to all and sundry you can now throw a ping-pong ball into the air and catch it on your nose.

1

You will, inevitably, be challenged to prove it. At this you start hedging. 'What now? Right here?' They will rise to the bait, especially when you take a ping-pong ball from your pocket and put it back again, as you say, 'No, you don't really want to see it. Take my word for it, I can do it.'

This will be met with a chorus of voices insisting that they won't take your word for it and they do want to see it done.

With feigned reluctance you take the ball from your pocket again. Have them stand back to make more room and ready yourself by adopting an appropriate stance. Gently throw the ball, underarm, into the air and attempt to catch it on your nose. Unfortunately you fail. You recover the ball before it hits the floor, throw it up and fail again.

'Those were just practice runs,' you say. 'Now I'll do it for real.'

And you do! **1** You throw the ball up and you catch it on your nose **2**. With your head back, and never taking your eyes off the ball, you keep it balanced by shifting from side to side in the time-honoured style of all great jugglers.

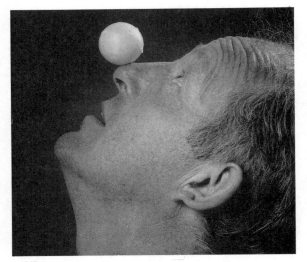

2

Your friends will be greatly impressed. You take your applause like the showman you are and then you straighten up and your head assumes its normal position and the ping-pong ball stays exactly where it is – stuck on your nose! **3**

The Secret

All you need is some clear pure rubber glue or cement. Copydex is perfect. Coat the ping-pong ball with the gum **4**. A very small amount

3

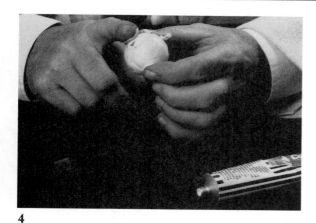

4

5

will suffice. Then with a fingertip run a line of gum along the entire length of your nose, stopping just under the tip **5**. Let both dry and you are ready to practise.

The only real ability involved is to get the ball to land on your nose. Actually it's so easy that after a few goes you'll have trouble missing.

Obviously you will only need to apply the glue to your nose a short time before you intend to perform. Don't leave the ping-pong ball on your nose for too long, only as long as it's funny. Once they've got the point of the gag, take it off and pocket it. Have fun.

One tip, use only a very small amount of glue. The photos show exaggerated amounts. And it's best to remove the ball in private, so as not to reveal the method.

MONEY-BOOK

Having gone to the expense of investing in a tube of rubber glue like Copydex for the last trick, we'll give you full value for your money with this amusing stunt.

The Effect

When it's your turn to pay for a round of drinks at the bar, you take from your pocket a flat chequebook holder and open it to reveal a stack of £5 notes neatly glued in place just like cheques.

You then peel one off, tear it out and settle the bill.

The Secret

Get twenty-five or fifty crisp new £5 notes from your bank. Cut out a piece of thin card the width of and just a little longer than the length of a £5 note. With a razor lightly score a line across the width of the card, very near to one end, approximately equal to the height of the stack of banknotes you will use. Turn the card over and fold the scored end up to form a lip. Cut a small piece of gauze to fit in the angle of the lip and the card. Glue it in place with your Copydex, then carefully butt the edge of your neat stack of banknotes into place while the glue is still wet. Let it dry, then insert the card into your chequebook holder and you're ready to go.

When you use it, just present it as though it's the most normal thing in the world for you to do, which by the end of this book it probably will be.

FINGER FUN

Here is a bit of silliness that's great fun in a bar situation or at a party. It's presented as a 'do as I do' effect by the magician. Spectators have to keep their fingers on their noses, as described below.

The Effect

The magician extends his arms, crosses them and clasps his hands together, fingers interwoven. He then brings his clasped hands inside and up and pinches his nose between his

1

3

forefingers **1**. Then he unclasps his other fingers, keeping his forefingers on his nose, and raises his elbows up and to the side **2**.

Some people copying these actions will be in exactly the same position as the performer; others will be hopelessly entangled, unable to unclasp their fingers **3**.

The Secret

If when you extend your arms and clasp your hands together your right thumb goes inside your left thumb, it will always work correctly **4**. If your left thumb goes inside your right thumb, it will be impossible to unclasp your hands. Curiously, many people instinctively clasp their hands together in the wrong position. That simple fact makes for a lot of fun.

2

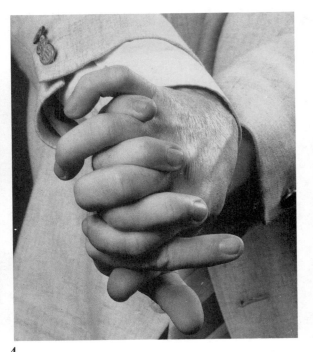

4

GELLERESQUE

This is a very entertaining and quite weird mini-demonstration of the power of the mind, ideal for performance in a bar setting.

The Effect

The magician very carefully balances two matchsticks on the edge of a matchbox. He then asks a spectator to choose one match for himself and one for the magician.

The magician explains to the spectator that this is a challenge demonstration of telekinetic power or, as the layman would better understand it, mind over matter. The magician states that they must both focus their total concentration on their respective matches.

Both concentrate fiercely. Suddenly the magician's match topples and falls. The spectator's match remains stationary.

The Secret

A magician's magic trick supply catalogue would probably advertise this trick as follows:

MIRACLE TELEKINETIC MATCHES

Demonstrate the power
of your mind to move inanimate objects
at your command! No magnets, threads,
confederates, motors, outside agencies
or gimmicks of any kind.
Can be done completely surrounded,
totally impromptu.
The miracle of the age.
Only 20p.
Sold as a sealed manuscript.
(Supply your own matches.)

Such an effusive write-up would not in fact infringe the Trades Description Act. The uncanny effect achieved is out of all proportion to the method employed. All you have to do is secretly dip about 3 mm (½ in) of the non-striking end of your match into your drink for thirty to forty seconds. Then take it out and wipe off the excess, visible liquid with your fingers.

To present the trick, stand a matchbox upright on its striking surface or top end, whichever is the most stable. Now very carefully balance both matches across the matchbox. The best way to do it is to hold the head of the match between your right forefinger and thumb and place it on the matchbox, then let go. Now, to achieve a very finely balanced position, put your right forefinger and thumb together and position them just under the head of the balanced match on one side of the box. And, with your left thumbnail, gently nudge the opposite end of the matchstick towards your right thumb and finger. If you push it too far the head will tip on to your right thumb and finger, which can then support the head of the matchstick and delicately ease it back a fraction **1**. I've found this to

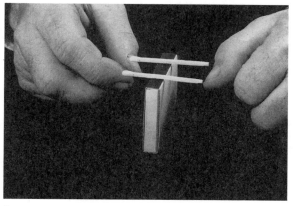

1

be the best way to get two matchsticks very finely balanced on a matchbox. This is important for the successful outcome of the trick.

Ask a spectator to point to one of the matchsticks. If he points to the one that you haven't dipped in your drink say, 'OK, that's your choice. So I'll have the other one.'

If he points to the dipped match, say 'OK, so that's the one I'll use. Now while I concentrate on it I want you to concentrate on the other one.'

In this way you have exercised a magician's choice. A nice variation on this, if he points to the dipped match, is to say, 'OK, we'll concentrate on that one and everybody else must concentrate on the other.' This approach directly involves everyone, which makes for good entertainment.

I've found that a spirit, such as gin or

whisky, works better than a beer or water. In case you were wondering, the principle of the trick is that as the end of the matchstick dries, as the spirit evaporates, the balance of the matchstick is changed. The weight of the head will cause it to fall. It happens slowly, but that actually helps build up the effect.

PAUL'S PENDULUM

Let me pose a question. What do American farmers, chicken eggs, mail order catalogues and fishing weights have in common? You'll never guess the answer so I'll tell you straight away. It's a pendulum. In the United States before the Second World War hundreds of thousands of pendulums were sold by mail order to farmers as sex detectors. For a dollar the purchaser received a piece of string with a fishing weight tied to one end. The come-on to the farmer was that if he held the pendulum over an egg the action of the pendulum would tell him if the egg would hatch a rooster or a hen. That knowledge enabled him to cull the rooster eggs and so produce many more laying hens and increase his profits. Sounds unlikely, doesn't it?

If you were to read a small ad these days offering a magic pendulum that would infallibly reveal the truth of what people were thinking, you could be forgiven for being sceptical. In fact the pendulum does betray a person's thoughts in response to direct questions in an uncanny way that seems quite magical.

The Effect
The magician puts two playing-cards face up on the table about 30 cm (12 in) apart. One is the ace of spades, the other is the king of hearts. A female spectator sits opposite the magician and is asked mentally to select one of the cards.

The magician then gives her a magic pendulum. He positions her so that her right elbow is on the table, the string is held by her fingertips **1** and the pendulum is suspended over the table between the cards.

'I'm going to ask you a question shortly,'

1

says the magician, 'to which the answer will be either yes or no. You will not answer vocally. The pendulum will answer for you. If the answer to my question is yes, the pendulum will swing backwards and forwards in a straight line. If the answer is no, the pendulum will swing around in small circles. Do you understand? Just nod if the answer is yes. OK, here we go. Are you thinking of the red king. If the answer is yes the pendulum will swing in straight lines. If no, small circles. Concentrate. Think yes or no.'

The pendulum slowly starts to swing backwards and forwards in a straight line. The answer is yes, so the magician turns the black ace face down. The spectator verbally confirms the pendulum's success.

The Secret
I have described a most basic presentation to demonstrate best this unusual principle. The reason the pendulum works is a combination of suggestion and response. It is known to psychologists as a psychomotor response. The suggestion that the answer yes will produce a back and forth, straight swinging movement induces an involuntary response in the partici-

pating spectator. Her brain is telling her yes; this triggers unconscious, imperceptible movements in the hand holding the pendulum, resulting in its movement. If she is thinking no, the pendulum would swing in small circles.

Many presentations are possible. It can be an amusing game for mixed company based on truth or lies. A coin can be hidden under one of three upturned cups, if the pendulum is held over each cup in turn. The magician asks the question 'Is the coin under this cup?' in turn, having suggested the pendulum will swing in a straight line for yes and small circles for no. The action of the pendulum will locate the coin.

Attractive pendulums can be purchased from shops specialising in astrological and psychic product supplies. Alternatively you can make one. A finger ring and a length of cotton thread will certainly work.

If you doubt the claims I have made for the magic pendulum I urge you to try it for yourself. Make one up. Your starting position is always to have the pendulum hanging as still as possible, then think yes for a straight back and forth motion or no for circles. You'll be amazed!

CHALLENGE BALANCE

This is the perfect bar stunt. You can do it. Nobody else can.

The Effect
The magician hands out single matchsticks to each spectator. He then challenges them to stand their matches upright on their right thumbnail and keep it balanced in an upright position.

Of course nobody can do it. But you can. Here's how.

The Secret
And this really is a secret. Rub the bottom end of the match against your teeth (the back teeth will probably prove best). This transfers to the end of the matchstick a little of the residual film on your teeth, which acts like glue to anchor

the bottom end of the matchstick to your thumbnail, enabling you apparently to balance the match upright on your thumbnail.

Don't do it for too long. If somebody wants to try it with your match, remove the film with your thumb and fingertips in the process of handing it to them.

I know it doesn't sound very spectacular. But it's a very nifty little quickie and worthy of your consideration.

SECOND STRIKE

The Effect
If you are a smoker you'll get some fun out of this. Place a cigarette between your lips, feel your pockets with both hands, reach into one and take out a box of matches. Open the box and remove a burnt match. Draw attention to this and the contents of the box, which are another half-dozen burnt matches.

'That's an irritating habit,' you say, putting the used matches back in the box. 'Still, what would a real magician do?' So saying, you close the box and promptly strike the used match on the box. The match flares into flame like a new match and you light your cigarette with it. Then you blow it out and drop it into an ashtray.

The Secret
You will need a box of matches, a razor-blade or pocket knife, a bottle of black indian ink. Prepare half a dozen matches by whittling them for about half their length below the head, so they have the distorted shape of a half-burnt match. Dip them, one at a time, into the ink for half their length. Then pop them, head down, in a glass ashtray. When dry the matches will have the appearance of a used match, yet when struck will light exactly like an unused one – which, of course, is what they really are.

In the presentation above, you focus attention on the match to set up the effect. But you can also do it without comment, especially if you have distributed the matches in various ashtrays around the room. Simply take one from an ashtray, strike it and light your cigarette. You'll be amazed at the response you get.

NO SMOKING CIGARETTE

Having lit your cigarette with a used match you proceed to demonstrate that it is one of the new 50 per cent less smoke brands.

The Effect

The lit end of the cigarette glows brightly as you draw heavily on it. Your chest has expanded to accommodate the amount of smoke drawn from the cigarette. Exhaling, you blow a copious amount of smoke into the atmosphere.

You draw heavily on the cigarette again. The glowing end provides evidence of your lung power. You exhale mightily once more and blow out – nothing. Not even a trace of smoke.

You continue to alternate between exhaling smoke and exhaling nothing, despite the fact that each successive draw on the cigarette is apparently identical.

You can demonstrate this phenomenal new product for as long as your lungs last or the spectators can still see you.

The Secret

If you lightly blow through the cigarette instead of drawing on it, the end will glow brightly. At the same time as you secretly blow on the cigarette, simulate drawing on it by expanding your lungs. The simplest way to do this is to lift your chest by raising your ribcage.

A packet of twenty cigarettes will provide the opportunity for sufficient practice so that both actions look identical to the spectator.

EVERLASTING ASH

The last item in this trio of cigarette stunts is a very effective visual con.

The Effect

Without drawing any attention to the cigarette you are smoking, the spectators' attention will inevitably focus on it. Why? Because you never knock the ash from the cigarette. You will end up holding a cigarette on which the ash has stayed in place for the entire length of the smoked cigarette.

The Secret

Get a darning needle and push it point first into a cigarette so that its entire length is hidden in the middle of the cigarette.

Look carefully at the end of the cigarette to make sure the end of the needle can't be seen.

Now you're all set to go. Light the cigarette and smoke it casually. Do not, I repeat do not, draw attention to the cigarette.

1

As the ash lengthens, the spectators will notice it. Ignore their reaction and pretend to be absorbed in the conversation. If you are seated at a table, you may find that somebody will push an ashtray under your hand in line with the cigarette to catch the ash 2. If that happens, casually transfer the cigarette to your other hand. It will drive them crazy. You can even

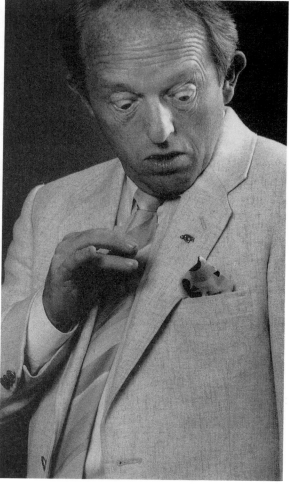

2

1

walk about holding the cigarette and the ash won't drop off.

Don't be tempted to let your friends into the secret. If you do it every once in a while you'll get a lot of fun out of it. Of course when it comes to disposing of the cigarette, you use one of the magician's indispensable allies – discretion.

CRAZY STUFF

Here two neat gags are combined to produce some funny business at the bar.

The Effect
The magician notices that the silk handkerchief in the outer breast pocket of his suit is jerking about in a crazy fashion. The spectators see it as well but also notice that his left hand seems to be pulling a piece of thread to operate the handkerchief movements. Their suspicion is dispelled when the magician takes the handkerchief from his pocket and hands it out for examination.

The Secret
All that's required is a small, lightweight silk handkerchief. Magicians' supply houses stock them in all sizes.

Tuck the ends of the handkerchief half-way into the pocket of your jacket so the centre section is sticking out. To make the silk move about, look down at it and blow on it through your nostrils in short bursts. The handkerchief will move about **1**. Varying the position of your head will create the effect of the handkerchief moving around.

Put your left fingers under the bottom edge of your jacket pocket and, with small movements, simulate pulling a connecting thread. The spectators will notice this and will think that you are operating the handkerchief movements, thus neatly diverting their attention away from the real method.

Obviously you must make your bursts of air as silent as possible. Don't prolong the effect. When you've got them hooked, take the handkerchief out of your pocket and hand it to

2

a spectator, saying, 'Must be the ghost of a silk-worm.'

When they hand back the silk handkerchief, you will be all ready and prepared to perform.

You take the silk handkerchief from the spectator and, crumpling it into a ball in your hands, throw it to the floor. From there it bounces straight back up about 2.5m (8 ft) into the air. You catch it and casually pocket it, as you say, 'I didn't like the colour anyway.'

The Secret

Crumpling it into a ball is almost correct. What you actually do is crumple the silk around a ball. Most toy shops and newsagents stock those super-bounce balls for children. They are available in a variety of colours. Select one that matches the silk as closely as possible.

The handling couldn't be simpler. Having passed the silk handkerchief around for examination, you casually put both hands into your trouser pockets. In your right-hand pocket you have the super-bounce ball. As you take the silk back with your left hand, remove your right hand from the pocket with the ball held in the finger palm position. Bring the hand straight up and crumple the ball in handkerchief so that there is only one thickness of silk over it. You can even subtly twirl the handkerchief so that the ball is secure **2**. This prevents the ball from separating from the handkerchief when you throw it to the floor and catch it after its bounce. With practice, you can catch it into your top pocket.

IT'S UP HIS SLEEVE

Two of the most overworked clichés applied to magic by the public are 'It's all done by mirrors' and 'It's up his sleeve.' In this trick the second one is appropriate, because you actually demonstrate this as a fact.

The Effect

You take a pen from your pocket and explain to your friends that you will let them into the real secret of producing things magically from

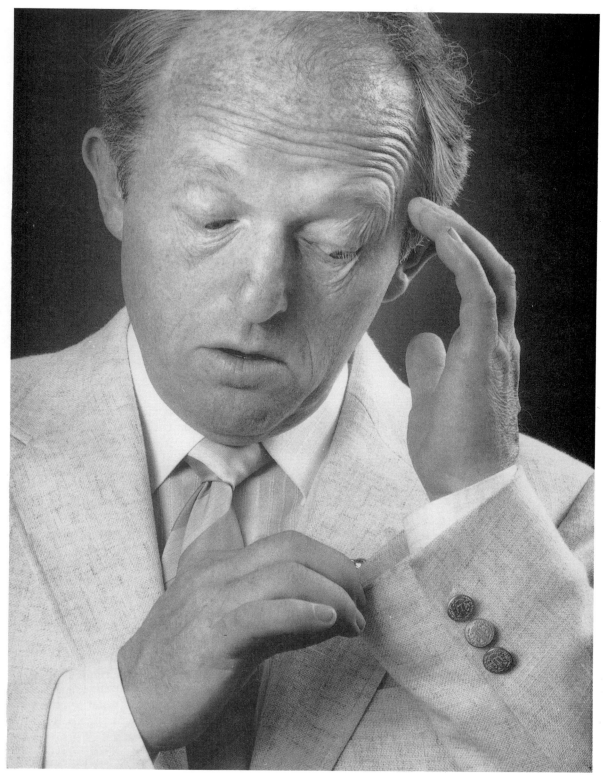

Paul thinking 'So that's where it went.'

your sleeve. 'You know how most people always think that magicians produce things from their sleeves. Well, actually it's true. Look i'll show you how it works.' So saying, you open your jacket by the lapel and put the pen into your left sleeve at the armpit **2**. Next you

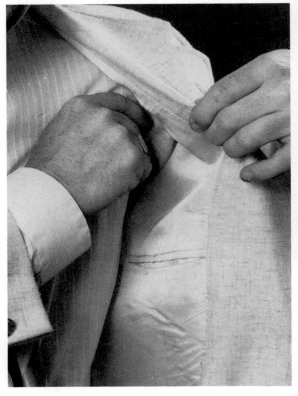

2

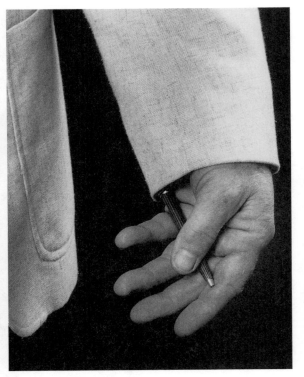

3

straighten your left arm down by your side and shake it. The pen emerges from the sleeve at the cuff into your cupped left hand **3**.

'That's the basic principle at work. The weight of the pen and gravity do it for the magician,' you say as you put the pen into the top of the sleeve again and shake it down into your hand.

'No big deal so far,' you continue, as you put the pen into your sleeve for a third time. 'But here is where a bit of conjuring technique comes into play. Once the pen is in the sleeve, I bend my left arm at the elbow and this keeps the pen in the sleeve until I'm ready to produce it.' You straighten your left arm again, allowing the pen to drop into your fingers, and produce it with a flourish.

'Now you can see the difference. Look. I'll do it again. I put it into the sleeve. Shake it down a bit. Bend my elbow and now I am ready to produce it any time I like. In fact you tell me when to produce it, and make sure you pay particular attention to the subtle way I get it into my hand without anybody being aware of it.'

Your friends tell you to produce the pen. Casually you lower your left arm to your side, then raise your left hand with a flourish and produce nothing! Somewhat puzzled, you try again, this time obviously shaking the pen down the sleeve and again raising your left hand and producing – still nothing!

'This is very embarrassing,' you say, as you try to produce the pen for a third time, quite forcefully shaking your left arm and shoulder and looking up the sleeve at the cuff. Still no pen, until: 'Wait a minute. What would a real magician do? He'd produce it from the other sleeve, wouldn't he?' So saying, you straighten your right arm by your right side, give a little shake and, presto, the pen drops from the sleeve into your right hand.

The Secret

Because this is such a nice little gag, I'll show you two methods of doing it.

Get two identical pens that have a little bit of weight to them. Clip one in your left inner jacket pocket. The other put into your right sleeve at the armpit and keep it in place with the inside of your upper arm. Practise walking around, gesturing, picking things up and putting them down with your right hand but keeping the arm bent a little. You'll soon discover that you can move the arm almost as freely as normal.

Practise the effect exactly as described. Take the pen from inside your jacket pocket, open your jacket so they can see you put the pen into your sleeve and shake it down into your hand,

etc. By the third time you do it you will have conditioned them into the sequence of moves. So don't open the jacket as wide and, although they don't see the pen go into the sleeve, they do see it come out. The fourth time you only pretend to put the pen into the sleeve. Simulate the moves you've made before but actually slip it into your inner pocket. The rest is pure presentation. When you are ready to produce it from your right sleeve, relax your right arm and let gravity do the rest.

The second method uses only one pen. Having gone through the first three moves exactly as described, on the fourth move, the simulation move, you actually bring the pen back flat against the palm and wrist of your right hand **4**. By swivelling the end of the pen

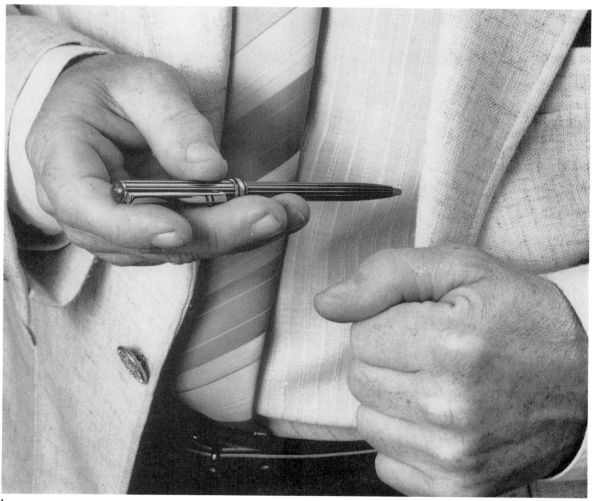

4

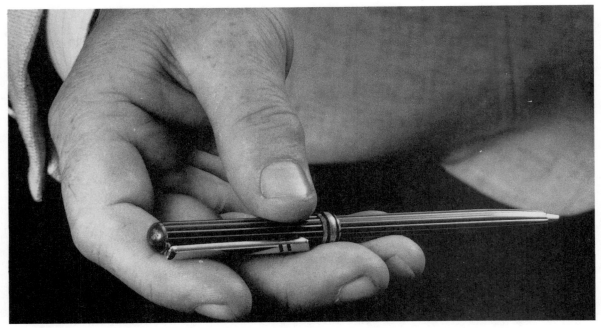

5

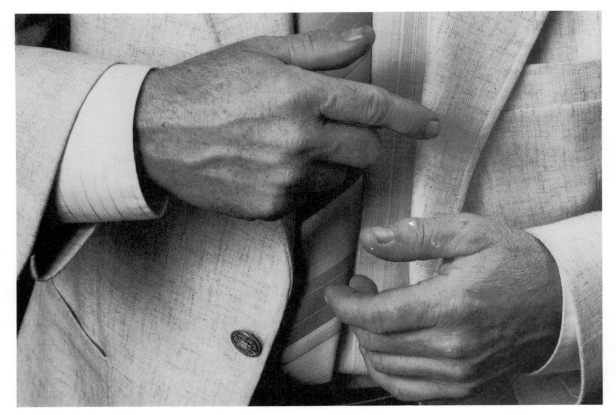

6

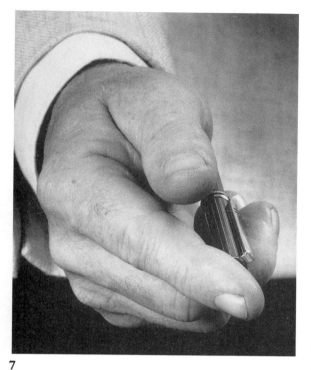

7

round between your thumb and first and second fingers **5** and clipping it against your palm with your second finger, you can remove your hand from inside your jacket without them seeing the pen **6**. Let your right hand relax and fall to your side. All attention is on your left arm at this point, so, provided you keep the back of your right hand facing forward, the pen won't be seen. Now, during your contortions with your left arm, you should find it easy to work the pen concealed in your right hand up part-way into your right sleeve **7** and **8**. At the moment of maximum audience attention on your left arm, raise your right arm into their air and lean to your left as though putting your entire body into the effort of making the pen appear from your left sleeve. This way you will have got the pen into your right sleeve without the audience being aware of it, and you're all set for the finish.

A little variation you might like to try is to produce the pen from behind your right knee instead of the sleeve. Practise it awhile until you get a sense of the timing and you'll have a lot of fun with this trick.

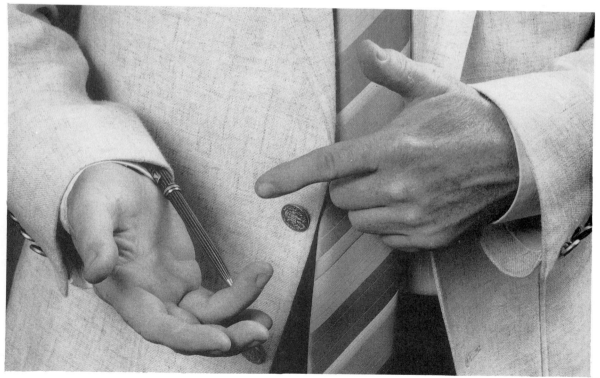

8

CHAPTER 7
SMALL WONDERS: THE ART OF AMUSING CHILDREN

The man who has lost his power of wonder is a dead man. – *Albert Einstein*

Adults tend, quite frequently, to bump up against the world of children. And it's a different world to ours. A child's innate ability to create fantasy and see wonder in everything is magical to behold.

I'm sure when you were young you were entertained by your father, or an uncle, who baffled you with some small item of wonderment. Do you remember that? Wouldn't it be nice if, some fifty years on, you are similarly remembered by somebody who is a child today.

FLY AWAY, PETER

Almost every young child will have heard this venerable little rhyme. I personally know a two-and-half-year-old who can recite the rhyme with the appropriate actions. This version brings a little magic to the rhyme and will enable you to entertain and communicate with probably the youngest audience you will ever encounter.

The Effect
This is performed at a table. The magician sticks two little squares of paper on the fingernails of his index fingers. He puts both fingers on the edge of the table and drops both hands below the table edge, so that the top joint of each finger is hooked to the edge of the table. All that is visible is the top of each finger with the little paper square stuck on the fingernails.

The magician recites the rhyme in time with the following actions:

Two little dickie birds
Sitting on a wall,
(*Both fingers are hooked on to the table edge.*) **1**
One named Peter,
(*Waggle right top joint.*)
One named Paul.
(*Waggle left top joint.*)
Fly away, Peter,
(*Right finger is waved up and down in one motion. When the fingertip is hooked on the table edge again, the paper has vanished.*) **2**
Fly away, Paul.
(*This is repeated with the left finger.*) **3**
Come back, Peter,
(*Right finger repeats waving motion. When the fingertip returns to the table edge, the paper square has returned.*) **4**
Come back, Paul.
(*This is repeated with the left finger.*)

The Secret
Follow the actions in relation to the rhyme. To make Peter and Paul vanish, swop each middle finger for the first fingers. At the top of the single waving motion, as the hand starts to come down, curl each index finger into the palm and extend each middle finger and hook them on to the table edge. The only thing to guard against are critical angles. Nobody is more disappointed than the child who sees how it is done.

Young children who know the original rhyme are enchanted by this version.

1 (exposed views)

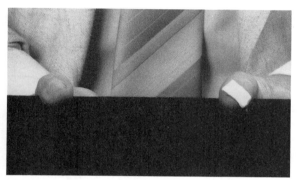

2

3

4

THE SHOOTING HANKY

Children are always keen to try things that impress them. So this little feat should go down well, because you can, if you wish, teach it to them.

The Effect

Holding a handkerchief by its opposite corners, the magician twirls it over and over until it's stretched taut. He takes aim with his left hand and shoots the handkerchief 4 m or so (13 ft) across the room.

The Secret

Hold the handkerchief by the opposite corners between your fingers and thumbs. Pay particular attention to your left index finger and thumb. The corner of the handkerchief is over the length of the pad (the fingerprint) of the thumb and is clipped to the side of the second phalange of the index finger.

Twirl the handkerchief between your hands until it tightens like a knarled twig, then, as you stretch it taut, extend your left arm and pull the handkerchief back over your left thumbnail and along the length of your left arm. You should be in a similar position to that of an archer drawing a bow.

Pull on the handkerchief with your right hand. At the same time your left hand turns back at the wrist and your left arm bends at the elbow **1**. Increase the tension on the taut handkerchief as you move both hands back in unison and then release the handkerchief with

1

your right hand a fraction of a second before you snap your left wrist and arm forward and let the handkerchief go. The handkerchief will shoot forward, horizontally, across the room.

It would be a little too glib to say practise it until you get the knack. It is a knack, but one that is dependent on feel, certainly with regard to the right amount of tension on the taut handkerchief, and timing, with regard to the release of the right hand and the snap-flick of the left wrist.

Your skilfulness at performing this trick can be judged by the distance you shoot the handkerchief. Properly worked, it can be quite spectacular, especially to small children. It is all the more impressive if you can name a target and actually hit it.

THE INVISIBLE HAIR

This is a charming little trick for children, highly visual, magical and entertaining.

The Effect

The magician pulls a handkerchief by its centre through his left fist so that it stands upright. He threads an invisible hair through its point **1**. When he pulls the hair, the point of the handkerchief bends in the direction the hair is pulled **2**. It is pulled back and forth a few times until the magician bites the hair in two, when the handkerchief, released from the tension of

1

2

the hair, snaps upright. The handkerchief is shaken open and can be handed out for examination.

The Secret

Look carefully at the second photograph. You can just see a little of Paul's left thumb, and this is what moves the handkerchief. With an absolute minimum of visible movement you will be surprised at how far you can cause the handkerchief to bend.

The business with the handkerchief is purely presentation. But if you practise your timing in the mirror to perfect the pulling, bending and straightening movements, you'll appreciate how good the effect looks. Like many things in magic simple methods should not be interpreted as unworthy of consideration. It is the effect that counts. The method is only a means to an end. As Stanislaw Lec once said: 'Simplicity is genius.'

LULU

One of the finest specialist monthly magazines for magicians in the world is *Genii*, which has seen continuous publication since its first issue in September 1936. The original editor and publisher was an American lawyer, William W. Larsen Senior, an inventive amateur. The following effect became synonymous with his name due to an amusing rhyme he wrote to accompany its performance. Sadly, the innocence of his original verse has been affected by changes in connotation that make it inappropriate for general use today. Such is progress.

I have taken the liberty of partly rewriting the rhyme. The delightful appeal and novelty of the presentation remains timeless.

The Effect

After tying a single knot in the hem of a man's

handkerchief and giving it a series of rapid twirls, the magician introduces Lulu from the *Folies Bergère* who performs to this accompanying rhyme:

> Lulu loves to dance all day.
> She bends her legs in a funny way.
> And if one flower you would pay,
> She goes ta-ra-ra-boom-de-aye!

As the magician speaks, the handkerchief dances and to coincide with the last line does a high kick, *Folies* style.

The Secret

There is no real secret to this effect other than the secret of good presentation. To prepare it, which you can do in front of the spectators, tie a single tight knot in the hem of a man's handkerchief **1**. Take the two corners furthest from the knot in each hand and vigorously twirl the handkerchief over and over until it constricts as far as it will go **2**. Then hold the ends of the handkerchief in your left hand. These are the legs. And the knot in your right hand becomes the head **3**.

Time your presentation as follows:

> Lulu loves to dance all day.
>   (*Exhibit Lulu as in photograph* **3**.)
> She bends her legs in a funny way.
>   (*Move your hands together and apart a couple of times.*)
> And if one flower you would pay,
>   (*Keep bending and straightening the legs.*)
> She goes ta-ra-ra-boom-de-aye!
>   (*Release one of the legs on 'boom'.*) **4**

One tip to remember is, the thicker the cotton of the handkerchief, the better the effect.

1

2

3

4

THE ANIMATED MOUSE

A magical pitchman is one who demonstrates a small, inexpensive trick with the purpose of selling it to the onlooker, who, sufficiently intrigued with the performance, responds with an impulsive purchase. Pitching magic is a highly skilled and specialized form of sales demonstration, which is largely dependent on the directly commercial appeal of the trick itself.

Probably the most famous pitchman's trick is the 'Svengali Pack'. An American, the late Burling Hull, is usually credited with its invention, although its provenance is not absolutely certain. The pack is gimmicked to produce a routine of dazzling effects, so impossible that even the most resistant sceptic feels compelled to purchase. Millions of packs have been sold over the years, pitched in the streets, in department stores and even on television. Unfortunately for Burling Hull, he never received a single cent in royalties.

Another big selling line in pitchman effects is the animated mouse. A small plastic mouse scampers freely over the demonstrator's hands without any visible cause. A recent variation on the mouse is the 'Squiggle', a short snake-like piece of material which can squirm through the demonstrator's fingers. This is very much a toy, with little attempt being made to present it as magic.

The precursor to the pitchman's animated mouse was the folded handkerchief mouse. A number of magical names have become synonymous with this cheerful little creation. It was a favourite effect of Charles Lutwidge Dodgson, who knew a thing or two about the ways of entertaining children.

Through all its manifestations, the appeal of the animated mouse has endured. It should be in your repertoire. All you need is a clean white handkerchief.

The Effect

The magician carefully folds a white handkerchief into a shape that resembles a mouse. It sits on the palm of his right hand where he gently strokes it. Slowly, magically, it comes to life. It

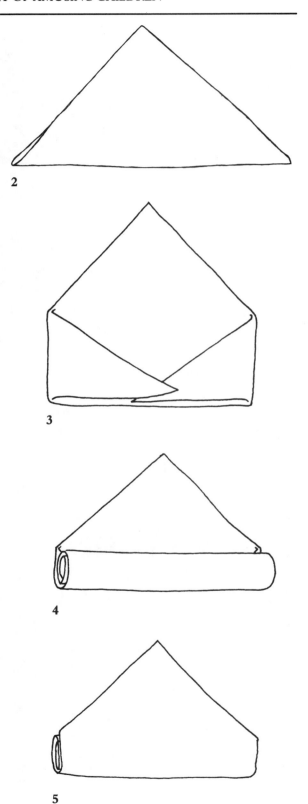

2

3

4

5

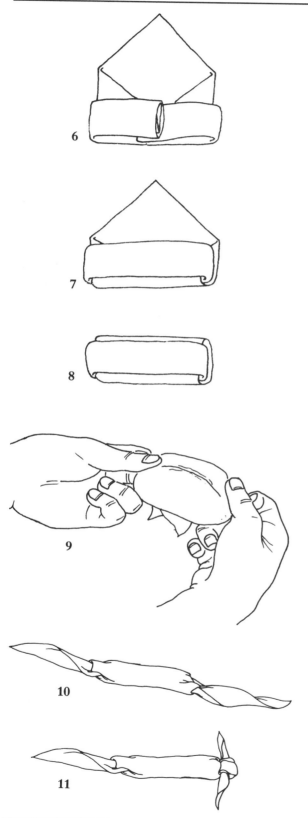

trembles, twitches, starts to move a little, it has to be gently restrained.

'This is Lewis the mouse. Would you like to stroke him?' says the magician to a child. It's an irresistible offer to a child, who will reach forward to do so. As her fingers touch the mouse, it suddenly takes off along the magician's arm. He has to grab it and pull it back to his hand, from where it leaps out again. A frantic chase ensues, the mouse running up and down the magician's arms, across his body, behind his neck, in his jacket until, finally exhausted by his antics, Lewis whispers to the magician that he wants to go to sleep in his favourite pocket. The performance closes as the magician complies.

The Secret

There are two aspects to the secret of the handkerchief mouse. One is the means of making it move and the body language that covers it. The other is the conviction and credibility which you give to acting as though the mouse were real. For that is what the child believes: the mouse has really come to life.

Let's start with the fold.

1. Lay the handkerchief flat on the table in a diamond shape.
2. Fold the point nearest to you up to meet the point furthest from you.
3. Fold the right and left corners of the triangle so they slightly overlap.
4. Roll the bottom edge up to about 10 cm (4 in) from the top point.
5. Turn the handkerchief over so the rolled part is on the table.
6. Fold the rolled ends up and in so they overlap.
7. Roll up again to about 4 cm (1½ in) from the pointed corners.
8. Lift the corners and tuck them firmly back into the roll.
9. Insert both thumbs into the bottom pocket of the rolled handkerchief and turn it in on itself. Keep rolling it inside out until two corners appear.
10. Tease the points out and pull gently.
11. To create two ears, spread out one end, hold either side of the point with both hands and twirl it over two or three

times and tie the ends you are holding together in a knot.

12. Put it across the length of your right hand so the ears are towards you.

13. Say hello to Lewis the handkerchief mouse.

Look at the first photograph and note that the tips of the right-hand first and second fingers are positioned at the end of the body, under the tail of the mouse. If you stroke the lower half of the mouse's body with the base of your closed left-hand fingers, you'll see that you are also covering the right fingertips **2**. This hides the fact that if you sharply snap your right second and third fingers in towards your palm, the mouse will appear to leap along your arm. If you gently nudge the mouse with the same two fingers, it will only move an inch or two.

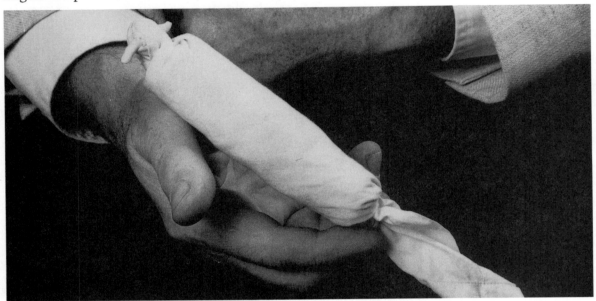

1

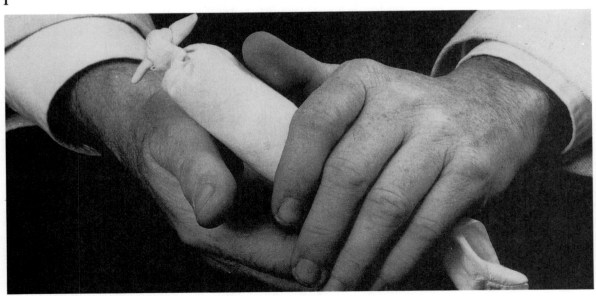

2

Those are the two basic actions to move the mouse in your hands. Making the mouse run up and down across your body **3**, and along your arms is achieved by actually pushing the tail end of the mouse's body with the fleshy base of the fingers, whilst simulating attempting to grab it with your fingers. Your upper body movements should simulate those you would make if you had a real mouse running over you – because that is what you are acting out: the pretence that you are trying to catch a live mouse.

If you introduce Lewis as a little mouse who can sometimes be rather naughty and has to be firmly kept in check by the magician, the children will love it when he runs out of control. They love to see authority flouted, especially by a mischievous mouse.

3

THUMB STUFF

Purely visual magic is often the most surprising magic, apparently proving that you can't believe your eyes. Here are a couple of marvellous examples.

The Effect

The magician appears to remove his thumb and put it back again. To further convince disbelievers, he promptly removes a fingertip and puts that back.

The Secret

Hold your left hand flat, the palm towards your body, with fingers and thumb together. Bend your left thumb inwards at the first joint, do the same with your thumb and butt your right thumb's first joint against the first joint of your left thumb. The first photograph shows an exposed view of this. Cover the 'join' of the two thumbs with your right first finger. It looks as though you are holding the first joint of your left thumb between your right forefinger and thumb **2**.

Now slide your right hand about 4 cm (1½ in) along your left forefinger and slide it back again **3**. Do this two or three times, then the last time, when the thumb is 'removed', quickly thrust it back as though you were forcing it back on. That's what it will look like. In fact you spring your left thumb straight and grip it at the first joint between your right finger and thumb in the actual grip you have been simulating. As soon as you grip the left thumb, shake it with your right hand as though testing its repaired strength.

Practise this in front of a mirror to perfect the illusion. When it looks deceptive to you, it will to the spectators.

A variation of this effect is to remove your middle fingertip. Hold your right hand flat, fingers together. Bend your middle finger in at

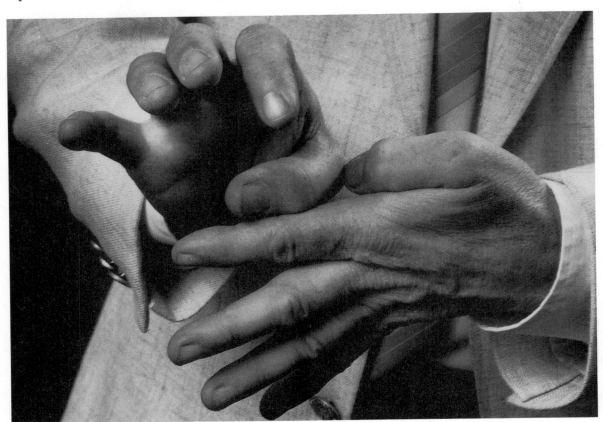

1 (exposed view)

the second joint, bend your left thumb at the first joint and butt it against your middle finger **4**. Cover with your left forefinger **5** and 'remove it', not quite as far as the fingertips **6**. Slide it back and forth a couple of times, repair it quickly and shake the join as before. The shaking adds considerably to the illusion. This little bit of finesse was passed on to Paul by the marvellous American magician Jay Marshall.

Paul does this effect beautifully and, if you practise, so will you.

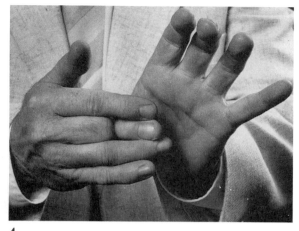

4

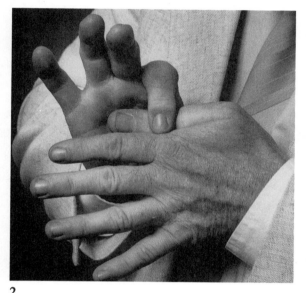

2

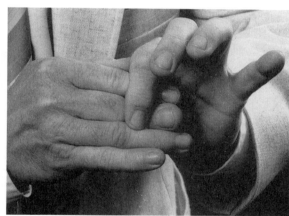

5

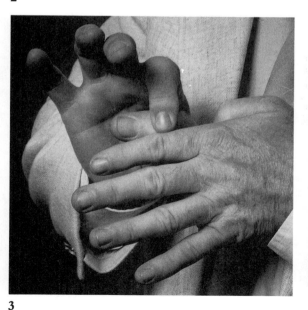

3

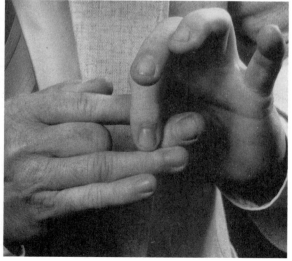

6

MONEY RING

If you want to give a child a cash gift or some pocket money, here is a novel way to present it to them. Have them hold out their hand and slip a ring made of money on to one of their fingers. Here is how to make one.

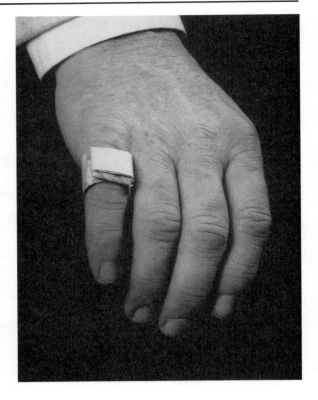

1. Fold about a fifth of the width of the note upwards and crease firmly **1**.
2. Fold the top of the note down and into the previous fold and crease **2**.
3. Fold the bottom edge to the top edge and crease **3**.
4. Fold a little more than about quarter of the left end of the strip up at a right-angle, crease **4** and wrap the right end of the strip around behind and over the vertical fold.
5. Fold the upright end of the strip down over the horizontal strip and fold it in and up **5**.
6. Fold the right end of the strip back and over, insert and tuck in.
7. All you need is a finger to put it on.

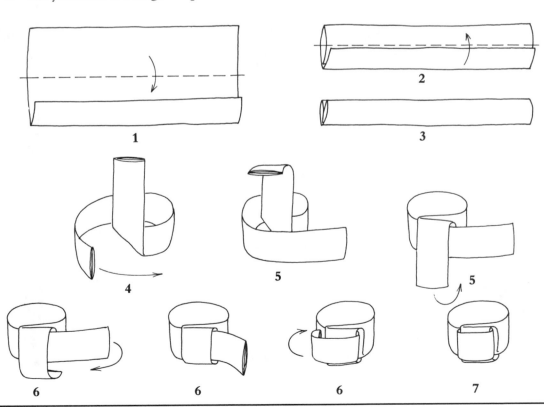

THE FLAPPING BIRD

Magic has a number of subjects related to it. One is the charming Japanese art of paper-folding called origami. A particularly pleasing example for children is the Flapping Bird.

Arts and crafts supply shops or the British Origami Society supplies list are sources for a wide variety of ready-cut coloured papers suitable for folding. Lighter, thinner papers are most often used, as they make quite strong, rigid models.

Begin with a piece of paper about 12 – 15 cm (5 – 6 in) square and fold a starting base in the following way.

1. Fold a vertical crease in the centre of the paper.

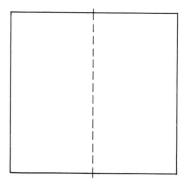

2. Unfold and then fold a horizontal crease, top edge to bottom edge, in a valley fold (a concave crease).

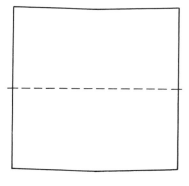

3. Fold the top right corner to the centre of the bottom edge, crease in a valley fold and turn the paper over 180 degrees.

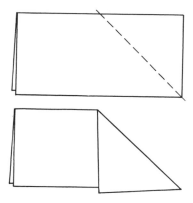

4. Fold the top right corner to the centre of the bottom edge, crease in a valley fold.

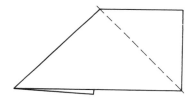

5. Put your thumbs inside and middle fingers outside at X and Y. Open the paper so points A and B meet and press model flat to make a square.

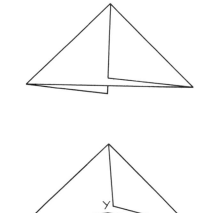

You are now all set to fold the model proper.

6. Fold points X and Y to meet at the centre crease Z.

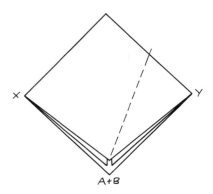

7. Turn the paper over and repeat.

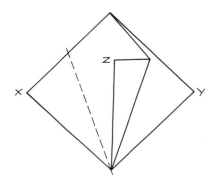

8. Fold the top point X down to Y, crease sharply and unfold it to position it was in before fold.

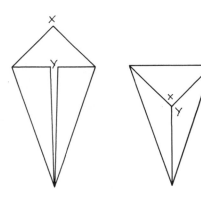

9. Unfold to the end of step 5.

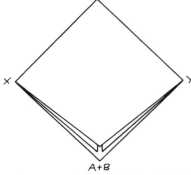

10. Fold point A up and X and Y in. This is a petal fold. Turn over and repeat.

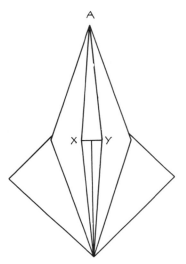

11. Fold right flap point A across to left flap point B. Turn over and repeat.

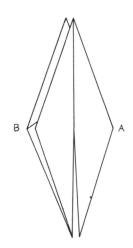

12. Fold bottom D up to meet top points E and F. Turn over and repeat.

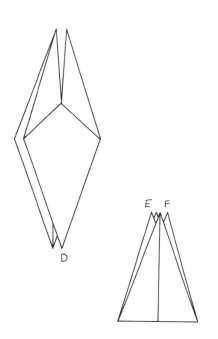

13. Pull points E and F one at a time, out and down about 45 degrees. Sharply crease bottom edge.

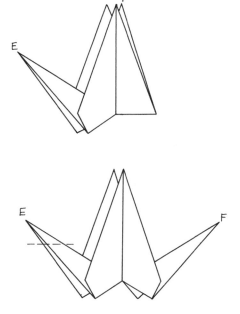

14. Reverse fold point E inside stem and crease for the bird's head.

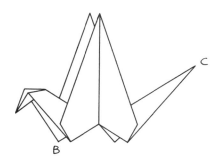

Curl the wings outward a little and hold the chest of the bird at B and gently pull the tail in and out in the direction it is pointing at C. The bird will flap his wings. Demonstrate this to the child and present her with the model for her further enjoyment.

CHAPTER 8
BASIC CARD HANDLING

If at first you don't succeed, you're running about average. – *M.H. Alderson*

Considering how many people enjoy playing card games for recreation, it's really surprising how few people handle cards with any degree of dexterity. I've seen card players who play regularly shuffle and cut the pack and deal the cards as though they were wearing thick woollen gloves and handling a stack of cheese sandwiches.

For a magician, it's doubly important that he handles cards well. It demonstrates accomplishment and also enables him to present his tricks smoothly, especially when he is performing some secret manoeuvre and doesn't want to draw attention to the cards.

A facility with card handling allows the magician to concentrate on the presentation of the trick and takes the heat off the things he doesn't want the spectator to notice.

The card–handling techniques in this chapter are by no means comprehensive in the field of card magic, but they do cover everything you need to know to perform the tricks in this book.

Practising doesn't mean slavishly grinding away in some locked room for hours on end. The techniques on offer here are all very simple and easy to acquire once you have a clear understanding of what you are learning and the positions your fingers need to be in. You will be able to practise anywhere, even while watching television. A little and often will prove more beneficial to progress than occasional marathon sessions.

STANDARD DEALING GRIP

This is the most common way of holding the cards. The left thumb works in unison with the right thumb and forefinger, pushing a card

over to be taken by the right hand. Practise for smoothness rather than speed. That will come with confident handling.

THE MECHANIC'S GRIP

The cards are held in deeper position in the hand, enabling the left index finger to curl over

the end of the pack. This alters the bias of the grip, allowing the other three fingers the freedom to move from the side of the pack which facilitates false dealing, such as a second deal or bottom deal. This grip is much favoured by card sharps, a mechanic being a specialist in false deals. Once you get used to it, it's a very practical grip.

THE RIFFLE SHUFFLE

Riffle rhymes with piffle and is an on-the-table shuffle much favoured by gamblers and good card-players. The reason is because, properly executed, it is impossible for anybody to glimpse the faces of any of the cards during the shuffle. The pack is cut into two halves **1**. The

1

2

original top half of the pack will be the right-hand portion. They are placed in an angled position on the table, so that when the thumbs

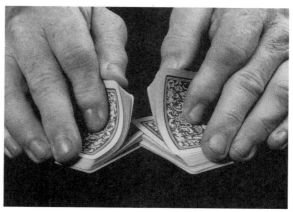

3

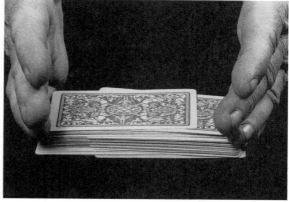

4

briskly riffle up the two top inner corners **2**the cards weave together as they are released by the thumbs **3**. When the riffle is finished, the cards are straightened and pushed together, using the third and fourth fingers of both hands **4**. The cards can now be squared up.

RETAINING THE TOP STOCK

During a riffle shuffle it is possible to keep one or a number of cards that were on top of the pack in that position. This is achieved by releasing cards in the left-hand half of the pack quicker, and by the right thumb releasing cards

Retaining the Top Stock

slower and releasing the top stock of cards in a block to complete the shuffle before squaring up. The fingers of both hands cover the cards during the shuffle to hide this manoeuvre.

RETAINING THE BOTTOM STOCK

By reversing the handling of the last technique you can keep the original bottom stock of cards in their position on the bottom, by simply releasing them as a block with the left thumb. The photograph shows an exaggerated view of this. The cards are then riffled and released by both thumbs, allowing the rest of the cards to weave together as normal. The cards can then be squared up.

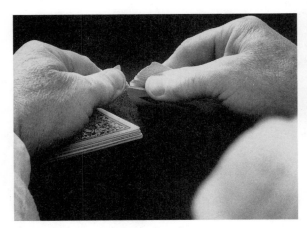

Retaining the Bottom Stock

THE WATERFALL SHUFFLE

This is a spectacular in-the-hands shuffle. If ever the expression 'a photograph is worth a thousand words' needed justifying, this shuffle proves it.

Hold the cards in the right hand, with the right index finger pressing on the back to create tension. The left hand is in position to receive cards **1**. Release half of the pack with the right

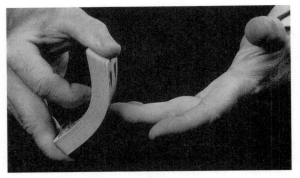

1

thumb, so the cards fall on to the left fingers, where they are gripped as a block with the left index finger on top of the block and supported by the right fingertips **2**.

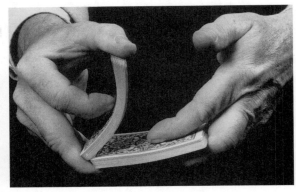

2

The left hand moves down as the right hand moves up, pivoting the cards up and allowing the left thumb to grip the edge of the packet **3**.

The middle, third and fourth fingers of both hands retain their grip on the cards as the hands

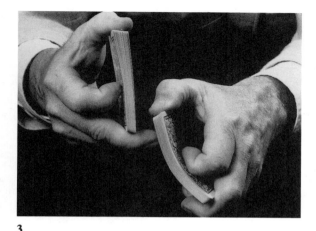

3

move slightly apart. Both thumbs can now release cards, in a riffling action, due to the tension on the cards, allowing them to weave together **4**.

4

5

When the weave is complete, both thumbs move to the centre of the top edges of the cards to prevent them from unweaving, as both hands bend the cards down and in, creating an arc shape as the fingers of both hands push up against the cards **5**.

By retaining the tension between the bases of both sets of fingers and thumbs, the cards can be held in this arc shape indefinitely. But, if you straighten the first and second joints of both

6

sets of fingers, the cards will fall and weave together with a satisfying purring noise **6**. When all the cards have been released, they can be squared up.

THE RIBBON SPREAD

This is often used to display the cards. Hold the squared-up pack face down in the right hand between the right thumb at the inner short end and the second, third and fourth fingers at the outer short end. The right index finger rests lightly against the left long side of the pack **1**.

The pack is placed on the table and spread from left to right in a sweeping movement. The right index finger is straightened slightly and the tip of the finger acts as a light brake to regulate evenly the spread of the cards **2**. The third photograph shows a completed spread. A card-table surface is very good for this type of display – and card work in general. A hard

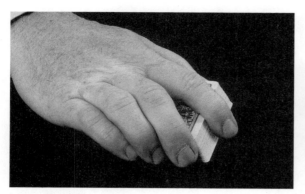

1 Star Position

2 Ribbon Spread – notice the even spread of the cards.

3 Completed Spread

surface makes most table-top card work difficult to perform satisfactorily.

THE RIBBON SPREAD PICK-UP

Position the right hand at the right end of the spread, fingers against the edges of the cards. Lift the edge of the cards at the end of the

spread **1** and, with the backs of your left fingers against the table surface, scoop them from left to right **2** and square them up.

1 Star Pick-Up

2 Pick-Up in Progress

THE RIBBON SPREAD TURN-OVER

This is really used as a flourish. If you rest the backs of your right-hand fingers against the top card at the right end of the spread, you will be in position to receive the cards, when, instead of the left hand scooping the cards up, it flips the left-hand cards over, resulting in the entire spread turning over like a wave in motion from left to right **1**. When the turnover is complete, the spread can be scooped up from right to left **2**.

A final nicety to this flourish is to pick up a single card with the right hand and, when you have commenced the turnover with the left

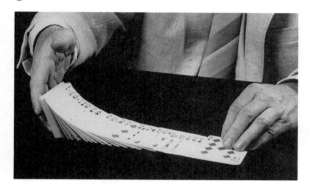

1

2

THE SWING CUT

This is a very neat in-the-hands cut. Hold the cards by the short ends **1**, between the right thumb at the inner end, slightly to the right of centre and the right second finger at the top right corner at the outer end. The right index

1 Start Position (see p. 90)

2 Notice Top Stock Pivoting against the Right Thumb (see p. 90)

3 (see p. 90)

3

hand, put the edge of the single card at a right-angle against the edges of the cards at the peak of the wave. You will actually be able to run the single card backwards and forwards along the spread, carrying the peak of the wave with it. It creates a very pretty effect **3**.

4 Left Hand Block Ready to be Squared-Up

finger will be able to lift up half of the pack and swing it as a block to the left, the block pivoting against the right thumb **2**. The cards are received in the crotch of the base of the left thumb and gripped there **3**. The right hand moves to the right and carries its block of cards out from under the left-hand block and, without any pause, places them on top of the left-hand block ready to be squared-up **4**.

THE SWIVEL CUT

Well executed, this is a very eye-catching fancy cut. The cards are held in the right hand in the same position as for the start of a swing cut, except the right index finger is curled on the back of the top card. The index finger of your left hand, whch is back upwards, pushes against the inner end of the pack, lifting and separating the block of cards from the rest of the pack **1** and in one continuous motion

1

swivels the block round in a 180–degree arc. The left index finger is pushing the block against the right middle finger, which acts as a pivot, during this movement **2**.

2

3

4

The arc completed, the block of cards will end up quite naturally in the left hand. The left index fingertip will be curled against the top outer end of the block **3**. The right hand carries its block of cards forward and drops them on to those in the left hand **4**.

UNDERCUT AND GLIMPSE

The swing cut and the swivel cut both transpose a block of cards from top to bottom. The undercut does the reverse. A block of cards is pulled from under the pack **1** and cut to the top.

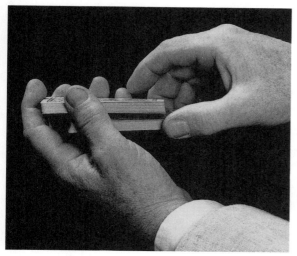

1

In the process of placing the undercut cards on top, it is possible to glimpse and remember the card at the bottom of the transferring block **2**.

2

The card then serves as a key card, particularly if you had a selected card replaced on top of the pack and undercut it to middle, apparently losing it in the pack. Of course your glimpsed key card would now be the card immediately above it.

FALSE CUT

This is a very simple yet effective from-the-hands-to-the-table false cut in which the order of the cards doesn't change. Undercut the bottom half of the pack **1** and place it on the

1

table **2** with the right hand, which immediately returns to the left hand and takes the block of cards and places them on top of the tabled block **3**.

2

Paul has a very deceptive additional touch during this cut. When his right hand returns to the left hand to take the remaining block, he butts the palm of his right hand against the inner end of the cards apparently to square them up before he puts them on top of the

3 (see p. 98)

4

tabled cards **4**. This type of finesse is called a feint, designed to divert the mind of the spectator as well as the eye. The fact that it adds 'a beat' to the move adds enormously to the deception.

THE CHARLIER PASS

This is a fancy one-handed cut which is very pretty. It was invented by a French magician called Charlier, ensuring him a permanent place in the magical record. The pack is held in the right hand as in the first photograph. Note that

1

2

3

the cards are held at an angle and pay attention to the position of the little finger. The second photograph is a side view of the same grip **2**. In the third one you can see how the right thumb has slightly lifted, allowing half the cards to drop on to the hand. The fourth photograph (p. 97) shows the right index finger pushing the cards up and against the ball of the right thumb.

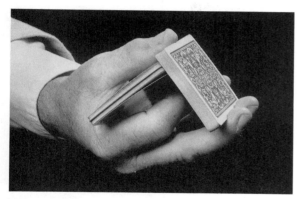

4 (see p. 96)

5

6

This action is continued, lifting the cards over the sides of the top block of cards, which drop and nest against the first phalange of the right index finger **5**. This finger now curls down, the resting cards going with it as the top block of cards close on top of them, rather like closing a book **6**.

Paul uses this as a finger exercise.

TOP CARD FORCE

This is a very bold card force, which is effective if you divert the spectators' attention by talking as you do it. Asking a question tends to make people look at the person being questioned, so timing is important.

The pack is held in your left hand. The card to be forced is on top of the pack. Our example in the photographs is the three of clubs **1**.

The right hand cuts off half the pack and puts

1 (exaggerated view)

2 (see p. 98)

3 (see p. 98)

4 (exaggerated view)

it on the table **2**. It returns to the left hand, takes the other half of the pack and puts it crosswise on top of the cards on the table **3**.

You now ask a spectator to take the card you cut to. The fourth photograph is an exaggerated shot showing the force card. In performance, as the spectator reaches for the card you lift the top half of the pack, allowing him to take the force card, which of course you will have remembered.

SHUFFLE GLIMPSE

This is a glimpse of the bottom card during an overhand shuffle. The short up-and-down movement of the right hand as cards are shuffled off is what makes this move deceptive. Most people who shuffle cards overhand shuffle them to both top and bottom of the left-hand

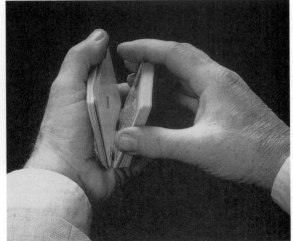

2

3

packet, as it is built up with cards being shuffled from the right hand.

Start by shuffling in the standard way **1**. Then at some point tip the cards in your left hand back in readiness to receive cards from the right hand to the bottom of those in your left. At the downward movement of the right hand, glimpse the bottom card of the left-hand packet **2**. In fact the right hand deposits no cards in the left hand. It hits the left fingers with its block of cards and immediately bounces up and continues the genuine shuffle to the top of the left-hand packet **3**.

The glimpse takes no more than a fraction of a second and is totally concealed by the action

1

of shuffling, so long as the rhythm of the shuffle doesn't alter.

If you do a genuine shuffle, then a second during which you shuffle glimpse, at the conclusion of the shuffle you have a key card in place ready to undercut on top of a selected card.

The author believes this subtle glimpse to be his invention but is steeling himself to hear to the contrary.

GAMBLER'S FALSE CUT IN THE HANDS

Hold the cards in the left hand in a Mechanic's Grip. FIG. 1. Undercut a third of the pack and slap it on top of the rest of the pack but protruding about 1 cm (½ in) over the outer end of the pack. FIG. 2. Undercut another third of the

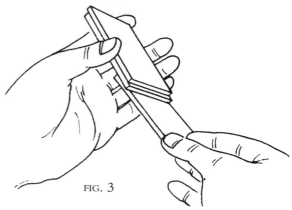

FIG. 3

pack and slap it on top of the protruding third. Undercut the final third of the pack FIG. 3 on to the cards in your left hand and square up. The order of the cards is unchanged. Practise this until you can do it smoothly and quickly and its deception will serve you well.

FALSE RIFFLE SHUFFLE OFF THE TABLE

This progresses in exactly the same way as the waterfall shuffle to the point where you riffle shuffle the cards together. But instead of weaving the outer ends of the cards together, you alter the position of the cards to a diagonal to make a V shape FIG. 1, so that only the two

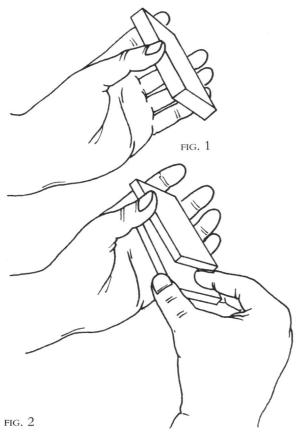

FIG. 1

FIG. 2

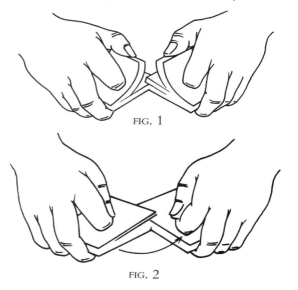

FIG. 1

FIG. 2

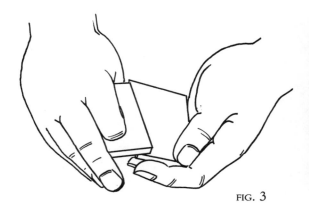

FIG. 3

1

inner corners of the cards, those nearest each other, weave together. You now close the V shape by bringing your hands together FIG. 2, your left fingers going under its cards, and the right hand remaining on top of its cards but pulling them up and over as a block on top of the left-hand cards FIG. 3. The effect of this is to disengage the weave and restore the pack to its original order. The best way to practise this is to do the shuffle legitimately, paying attention to the detail of the movements of both hands and the cards. Notice how you square the cards, because it is a legitimate shuffle you are attempting to simulate. This is not an easy false shuffle to master. But the more you practise, the easier it will become.

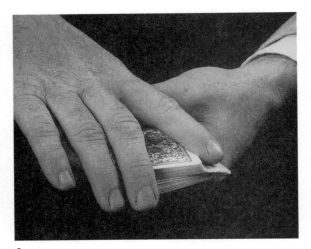

2

FANNING THE CARDS

Fanning cards neatly is a sign of practised handling and tends to establish the performer as a magician in the eyes of his audience.

Hold the cards in the left hand as in the first photograph, not too tightly. With the right-hand forefinger, pull the cards from the outer top left corner **2** in a crescent shape **3**. When the fan is complete, it will be gripped between the thumb on top and the fingers underneath. The index finger may well be pulled back so the second joint is pointing down: There is no absolute rule about this, as it varies from person to person. Fanning the cards is about feel and touch as much as anything else. The objective is to fan the cards so they are evenly spaced.

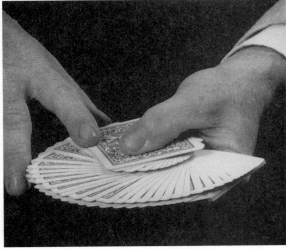

3

THE PRESSURE FAN

Hold the cards as in the first photograph. Then press the outer end down and in, bowing the pack up **2**. Maintain pressure as you simultaneously twist the hands in opposite directions **3**. The effect is that the cards are spread evenly in a fan **4**.

The only way to get the feel of this and to acquire the knack is by practising.

A final tip is to suggest you purchase some zinc stearate from a chemist and apply a little to each card. It will help you make super fans.

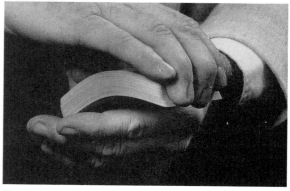

2

1

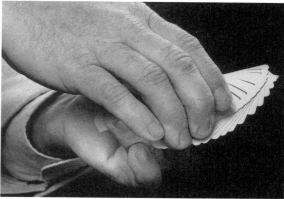

3

4

CHAPTER 9
MIRACLES AT THE CARD TABLE

Hereby you shall seeme to worke woonders. – *Reginald Scot*, The Discoverie of Witchcraft, *1584*

Probably the only modern interactive utility device that can claim to truly rival a pack of cards is a computer. And cards have been interesting for very much longer. Although nobody knows for certain where they come from, the link with ancient divinatory arrows and sticks seems plausible.

The arrival of playing–cards in this country is not documented. There is no mention of cards in *The Canterbury Tales* and, given the social mix of that gregarious band of pilgrims, it's reasonable to assume there was no widespread use of cards.

The first mention of conjuring tricks with cards in print was in Scot's *The Discoverie of Witchcraft*. What we will never know is the name of the first person ever to have created a magic trick with cards.

WITH A BORROWED PACK

Well-constructed magic tricks employ not only basic, functional conjuring methods to mis-direct the eye but also clever and subtle psychological techniques designed to divert the mind.

This compelling trick is a perfect example of the potency of this combination when presented with a modicum of underplayed showmanship. You have to sell the trick, but the audience should not be aware of that sell. That may well be the essence of all salesmanship. It is certainly one of the factors of showmanship. You will find this a marvellous effect to perform at the card table.

The Effect
Borrowing a cased pack from a spectator, the magician removes the cards and gets a spectator to shuffle them thoroughly and then to cut the pack into a line of seven approximately equal piles.

The magician then hands the spectator a pen and paper and asks him to list a column of numbers from one to seven. Against each number the spectator will write the name of the top card of the appropriate pile as the magician calls them out. But first the spectator must circle any one of the numbers on his list. The magician starts turning up and calling out the names of each card on top of the seven piles **1**.

1

The spectator writes the values of each card against its pile number. When this is done the spectator reassembles the pack and shuffles it. The magician takes the cards, cuts the pack in half, turns one half face up and shuffles it into the face down half. This mixed up pack is cut into two halves, the closed card case is put on top of one half and the other half is put on top

2

3

of the card case. This unusual card sandwich is then put into a handkerchief **2** and is vigorously shaken. The whole mixed-up mess is then tipped out on to the table **3**.

The magician asks the spectator for the name of the card written against his selected number. With his fingertips he picks out the card case and shakes it. It rattles. He opens the case and takes out a single playing-card. It is the spectator's card! **4**

The Secret

The success of this trick rests on one of the oldest, and possibly most under-used, principles in card magic. The way it is utilised here is particularly cunning. The description of the effect is exactly how they will recall it happened. But what you will have done is misdirect the possibility of their suspicion by simultaneously occupying them with something to do and using repetition to lull them away from the moment that makes the trick possible. That comes when you tell a calculated

white lie, because you miscall the name of a card during the performance.

Borrow a pack and, as you remove the cards, glimpse the bottom card and leave it in the case, remembering the value of this card. Put the pack on the table and close the card case. So now, unknown to your audience, the card case contains a single card which for our working example we'll call the ten of spades.

Get one of the spectators to shuffle the pack and cut it into seven approximately equal piles. Give him a pen and paper and have him write numbers one to seven in a column. Then ask him to circle one of the numbers; for our example number 3 is circled. Tell him as you call out the number of the top card of each pile in turn. He is to write it against the appropriate number. Now we come to a very important move. Whatever number is selected will be the pile when you miscall the name of the top card. So to draw attention away from that, you must miscall later in the count rather than earlier. The logic of this is to induce a sense of

4

monotony to the process of repetitiously naming the cards. If number 3 is circled, you would start pile number 7 on your left and progress to your right. This means that pile number 3 is the fifth pile called. So you would pick up the top card on number 7, casually showing the face of the card as you name it, for example, 'Pile number 7 is the queen of hearts.' They write this against the number 7. Replace the card face down on the pile.

'Pile number 6 is the four of clubs.' Pick up the top card of pile 6 as you talk and casually half show its face, replacing it on the pile.

'Pile number 5 is the three of diamonds.' Pick up and casually look at the card but don't show its face to the spectators. Replace it. What you are doing here is calling out the cards' names. The bias is towards calling, not showing.

'Pile number 4, the nine of clubs.' As you pick up and look at the card, casually replace it. Look at what they are writing. That is what is important – time the picking up, looking at and naming each card to the tempo of their writing. Time it so that, as they finish writing one card, you are calling another. So far, in a slightly monotonous fashion, you have correctly named each top card.

'Pile number 3, the ten of spades.' Pick up

the card, look at it and, no matter what it is, miscall it the ten of spades. Replace it on the pile. Do it in exactly the same way as you did the others. In the same voice, at the same pace.

'Pile number 2, the ace of hearts.' Pick it up, look at it, don't show it, replace it. You are back to correctly naming the cards.

'And pile number 1, the seven of diamonds.' Pick it up. Look. Replace it. All this is done at the same tempo. Seven piles enables you to establish that steady rhythm.

The spectators have been preoccupied writing. Nothing has apparently occurred, yet the trick is done. If they had called and circled number 6 on their list, you would have made pile number 1 the extreme right-hand pile to your right, their left. Your objective is always to name the miscalled card as far into the count as possible. If they circle number 7, start number 1 at the opposite end and, if 1 is circled, vice versa.

From here you proceed with the shuffling the card-case sandwich, mixing them up in the paper bag or handkerchief if no bag is available. You pick up the card case, shake it, open it, take the card out face down. Ask what card was written against their circled number, then turn the card face up.

THE ALL FAIR MIRACLE

If you could do real magic with a pack of cards, you would be hard pushed to present anything that could top this brilliant trick.

The Effect

The magician removes a pack of cards from its case and ribbon spreads them face up, calling attention to the fact that the cards are thoroughly mixed and are all different.

'Is that all fair so far?' he asks as he squares up the cards. The spectators agree and one of them is given the pack to hold behind his back and cut as many times as he likes. When he has completed this, the magician asks him to take three cards from the top of the pack and put them into his pocket without looking at their faces. 'Is that all fair so far?' The spectators agree. The magician then takes the pack and puts it back face down into its case and places it to one side.

'You will have noticed that I didn't even give the pack so much as a glance and I couldn't possibly know what cards were taken. Is that all fair?' The spectators agree on its fairness.

The magician then takes from his pocket a second pack that has a contrasting back design to the first one. After removing them from their case, he ribbon spreads the cards face up, showing them as freely as he did before. Squaring the cards he takes them behind his back and cuts them three times as the spectator had earlier done. He then removes three cards and places them face down on the table.

'As you've seen, I have exercised a free choice, as did my assistant. Would you agree that everything has been above board and all fair so far?' he asks. The spectators agree. This is the cue for the magician to ask the spectator to take his three selected cards from his pocket and place them face down on the table. Both now turn their cards face up. The magician's three cards are seen to be the same as the spectator's three chosen cards!

The Secret

You will need two packs of cards. Shuffle one pack, then spread it out in a wide spread so that you can see each card's value. Then assemble the second pack in exactly the same order as the first. This will give you two packs whose cards are stacked in identical sequence from top to bottom. Put one pack into its case. This pack we will call pack A, which will be the one that you will use. You pocket it. Take the card case of the second pack, pack B, which the spectator will use, and in the lower right-hand corner of the card case cut a small rectangular hole of sufficient size to allow you to see clearly the indice of a card when the pack is in the case. Cut the hole in the non-flap side of the card case, that is the side that the flap tucks into. Put the cards into this case and pocket them.

To present the effect, tell your audience that you are about to show them the fairest trick they will ever see. As you are talking, take pack B in its gimmicked card case, from your pocket, taking care to keep the side with the hole in it covered by your fingers or thumb. Remove the cards from the case and put the empty case, hole side down, on the table. Ribbon spread the pack face up on the table but keep your right hand over the last card of the spread. You are not particularly trying to hide it; you just don't want the card to register with the spectators. Apparently all you are doing is pointing out that the pack is all different and well mixed. Square the cards up and hand them to a spectator with the instruction to cut the cards behind his back a few times, then to take three cards from the top of the pack and pocket them sight unseen. Tell him to hand you the pack face down, emphasizing that this is because you don't want to see the faces of the cards. Put the pack into the gimmicked card case face down, below everyone's eye level, so that the bottom card of the pack is facing towards the hole in the card case **1** (p. 106). Then, as you tuck the flap in, turn the case towards you **2** (p. 107). This is a perfectly natural move and allows you to see the indice of the bottom card of the pack **3** (p. 107) in the most subtle way. Remember this card. For our example we'll say it's the three of clubs. Put the pack in your pocket and from a different pocket take out pack A. Remove the cards, cut them once or twice face down and ribbon spread them on the table, pointing out how well

1 (see p. 105)

mixed they are. A little point of finesse here is to put the card case on the table flap side up, as you did with pack B. This presents a continuity of action which subliminally doesn't jar on the spectator's consciousness. Such fine details make for fine magic.

Now we come to the all important move in the trick. Whilst pointing out the random mix of the cards look for and locate the card that was on the bottom of pack B. Our example is the three of clubs. The three cards immediately above or on top of it in the spread will be the spectator's selected cards. What you have to do is gather up the spread and hold the pack behind your back in such a way as to cut the three of clubs to the top, placing the three selected cards on the bottom of the pack so that you can draw them off and place them face down on the table. The simplest way to do this is, as you gather the cards, to break the pack above the three of clubs and place the top half under the bottom half in the act of squaring the edges of cards on the table top. The faces of the cards will be towards you, so if you do it quite casually whilst talking it should go unnoticed. Two other ways to do it are either to pull the three of clubs down a little and put the cards behind your back relatively unsquared – you

will be able to feel the three of clubs and cut it to the top – or you can in the process of squaring the cards insert your left little finger above the three of clubs as you loosely hold the cards in dealing position in your left hand before putting it behind your back where again you can easily cut to the three of clubs.

Try each of these different methods in practice to determine which is the best for you. Take your time about sighting your key card, in our example the three of clubs. Remember you are pointing out that the cards are well mixed and all different, so it's perfectly natural for you to be looking at them. You can even sort through them to separate them as you look for your key card. Magic is full of these types of subtlety where, whilst ostensibly pointing out or demonstrating one thing, you are really achieving something else.

All you need to do now is bring out the three matching cards and lay them face down on the table. Have the spectator take his cards from his pocket and lay them on the table. When the cards are turned face up they will match. The repetitive 'all fair' patter theme adds to the presentation as you are apparently demonstrating absence of trickery, whereas we know that you are really doing the exact opposite!

2 (see p. 105)

3 (see p. 105)

Signed Coincidence

SIGNED COINCIDENCE

Not everybody will do this trick, because there is a price to pay, but those who do will have added a stunning mystery to their repertoire.

The Effect

The magician shuffles a pack of cards and has a spectator cut the pack into two halves. The spectator takes one half, the magician the other. Each selects a card from their own halves and writes their signatures across the face of their card without the other seeing the cards. Each shuffles their signed, selected cards back into their half-packs, then each chooses a face-down card from the other's half-pack and shuffles them sight unseen into their own half of the pack. Both now ribbon spread their cards face up on the table and name their signed selected cards. Astonishingly the spectator's signed card is in the magician's spread of cards and the magician's signed card is in the spectator's spread of cards. Each drew and exchanged the other's signed card. What are the odds against that happening if there weren't a magician around?

The Secret

A little secret preparation prior to performance is necessary. On the back of the four of hearts make two pencil dots. Put one at the upper left-hand corner and one at the lower right-hand corner on the white margin of the card **1** – just

1

2

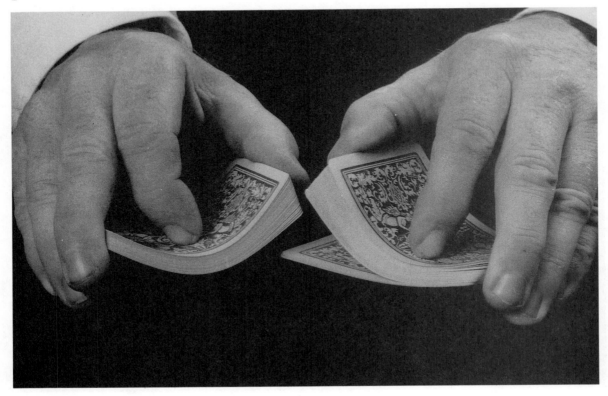

3

a small dot with a soft lead pencil that you can clearly see at a glance and which isn't obvious to anyone else will suffice. On the face of the four of hearts, boldly write your signature across the card with a pen. Then place it, face down, second from the bottom of the pack **2**.

To perform, you can safely riffle shuffle the cards by letting the bottom four or five cards in your left hand drop before you begin to release the right-hand cards **3**. Then ask the spectator to cut the pack into two halves and have him point to either half. What you are going to do here is force him to take the bottom half of the pack, which has your prepared card hidden second from bottom. To achieve this you resort to Magician's Choice which, like Hobson's Choice, really is no choice, although he thinks it's a free choice. If he points to the original bottom half, say, 'That's your choice. OK, pick it up and I'll take this one.' If he points to the original top half, pick it up and say, 'OK, you've chosen this for me, now pick up yours.' Either way it's the same difference; he gets the bottom half of the pack.

Ribbon spread your cards face down on the table and get him to do the same with his cards. Push one card out of the centre of your spread and have him do the same. Square up your cards and make him do the same with his. Tell him to write his signature on the face of his card and put it face down on top of his cards. While he actually writes his signature you only pretend to write yours. When you're finished, put your card on top of your half-pack and cut it three times. He does exactly the same, which will place his signed card two cards below your prepared card. Cutting three times ensures that these cards will be towards the centre of his half-pack. This is important because you now both ribbon spread your cards on the table. Get him to take any card from your spread and, without looking at it, put it into his; you must appear to do exactly the same. What you really do is sight your prepared card with the pencil dot and take out the second card along from it, counting to your right; this is his signed card **4**. Transfer it into your spread without looking at it, gather up the cards and shuffle them. He does exactly the same with his cards. You now ask him to name his signed card. He does so and you name yours – the four of hearts. Now ribbon spread your cards face up; he does the same. In his spread will be found your four of hearts – where it has been all the time, and his card will be found in yours. This is a pretty astounding climax.

4

ARE YOU SURE?

A peculiar quirk of human nature is the enjoyment of others' misfortune. Magicians have capitalized on this trait with the presentational concept of 'the magician makes good' in which a number of unforeseen errors creep unexpectedly into the conjuror's usually assured presentation of the trick. The spectators enjoy his increasing discomfort, only for the magician to turn the tables and triumphantly bring the effect to a successful conclusion, when they realise they have been led well and truly up the garden path.

In magical parlance this is called a sucker trick. It calls for a little of that latent acting ability I'm sure you have. If you can present it with the right amount of aggrieved disbelief as things go wrong, concluding with a modest smile of victory, you will have the right balance for an effective presentation.

The Effect
A spectator shuffles the pack while the magician's back is turned. He is instructed to think of any number between one and ten, then, without changing the order of the cards, silently to count down to the card at that position, look at it and remember it. The pack is handed to a second spectator who is asked to think of a number between eleven and twenty and to count down to it, again without changing the order of the cards, and remember the card at that position.

The pack is given, face down, to the magician behind his back. He turns to face the spectators. 'You won't believe this, but I'm going to find both your cards behind my back. I'll start at the beginning, which is always a good place to start, with the first card.' At this he brings the cards from behind his back. In one hand is the pack, in the other a single card.

'This is your card,' he states, with an air of slightly superior certainty to the first spectator. This gives way to a crestfallen 'It's not? Are you sure?' on being told that it's not the right one.

The magician seems puzzled for a moment, before he snaps back into action with a confident 'I'll tell you what I'll do. I'll use the first card to find the second card. What number was it at?' On being told

from the top was your card?' On being told seven, he counts and deals six cards face down on to the table and turns the seventh face up. 'And the seventh card is your card. Now what I'll do is . . .' By this time the first spectator will have pointed out that this is not his card either.

'It's not? Are you sure?' The spectator's certainty contrasts with the magician's puzzled discomfort as he slowly puts the seven cards on to the bottom of the pack. With a suspicious glance at the first spectator he turns to the second with a conspiratorial smile. 'We'll find your card first, instead. What number was it at?' On being told thirteen, he counts twelve cards aloud starting at eight, as seven are already face down on the table. 'And so the thirteenth is your card,' he says turning it face up with rather reduced confidence. The spectator informs him that it isn't.

'This is not your card? Are you sure?' He looks at the thirteenth card in disbelief. 'I'm sure I read the instructions properly,' he mutters to himself, as he puts the packet of thirteen cards face down on to the bottom of the pack. 'I can't understand it,' he says to the spectators as he riffle shuffles the pack.

'Cut the cards,' he says, offering the pack to the first spectator, who cuts off a portion of the pack. 'Put it on the table,' he instructs, as he casually places the balance of the pack crosswise on top of the tabled cards.

'Are you sure they weren't your cards?' he asks somewhat ruefully. 'Then these must be.' He turns the top half of the tabled pack face up and turns over the top card of the bottom half of the pack. His amused smile greets the spectator's confirmation that he is right.

The Secret
When both spectators have counted to and remembered their cards and given them to you face down behind your back, you turn to face them.

Whilst you are telling them how you are going to find their cards behind your back, take one card from the bottom of the pack and put it face down on top. Then take another card from the bottom and bring it out from behind your back and announce it as the first selected card.

When you are told it isn't, casually place it

face down on the bottom of the pack. Ask for the number their card is at. Our example is seven. Deal six cards singly face down in a pile on to the table and turn the seventh card face up. This isn't the selected card either. Do the 'Are you sure?' routine as you casually put the seven cards face down on the bottom of the pack. Unknown to the spectators, the first card is now the top card of the pack. Pick up the count at eight and deal it on to the table and continue dealing until you reach thirteen. Turn this card over. It won't be the second spectator's card. But the top card of the rest of the pack will be. Turn the thirteenth card face down and put it on top of the pile on the table and then put the pack in your hands on top of the pile on the table.

The condition of the pack is that, unknown to the spectators, their selected cards are now on the top and bottom of the pack. You now riffle shuffle the pack on the table, taking care not to let them see the face of the bottom card, in the following way. Release a few of the bottom cards of the left-hand packet first as you shuffle. And release the top few cards of the right-hand packet last as you shuffle. (See page 90.)

With the pack in your left hand get a spectator to cut the cards anywhere where they like and put them on the table. You then place the remaining half crosswise on top of the tabled half of the pack. In this way you have positioned both selected cards together in readiness for the climax of the trick, in which the spectator has, apparently, cut to the missing selected cards.

Although the mechanics of the trick are simple, presentation is everything. Over a century ago the famous French magician Robert Houdin was of the opinion that a magician was an actor playing the part of a magician. This is apt not only for this trick but for all the magic you perform. Think of it as playing a part. Visualize how you would like to project yourself in your presentations and then work towards those objectives. It can all be achieved if, in modern parlance, you go for it.

Houdin's original observation was made in the context of a reference to a performer's overt display of sleight of hand. Its wisdom is still applicable.

'A conjurer is not a juggler; he is an actor playing the part of a magician; an artist whose fingers have more need to move with deftness than with speed. I may even add that where sleight of hand is involved, the quieter the movement of the performer, the more readily will the spectators be deceived.'

Houdin was, of course, the namesake of Harry Houdini, who simple added the letter i to make it his own.

YOU ARE MAGIC

Here is a very puzzling four-ace revelation that requires four spectators and some neat handling on your part. It is the creation of the legendary magician Dai Vernon.

The Effect

The magician openly removes the four aces from a pack and puts them face up on the table. He holds the rest of the pack behind his back and, taking each ace in turn, inserts them into the pack. Bringing the pack from behind his back, he states that each ace is individually distributed somewhere in the pack. Next he has the first spectator cut off a small packet of cards which are turned face up and replaced on the pack. The magician spreads through the face-up cards until he reaches a face-down one. He takes off the face-up cards and puts them on the table. Then he takes the top face-down card from the pack and places it face down on top of the face-up packet on the table.

A second spectator cuts off a small packet of cards. The magician replaces them face up on the pack, runs through them until he reaches a face-down card and places the face-up cards on the table. The face-down card is dealt on top of them. The magician follows the same procedure with the third and fourth spectators. At this point there will be four face-up packets on the table, with one face-down card on each. The magician is holding the remainder of the cards in his hand, as he explains that this random cutting and sorting by each spectator has produced an effect that proves 'you are magic'. He asks the four spectators each to turn over one face-down card. They do so, reveal-ing the four aces! 1

1

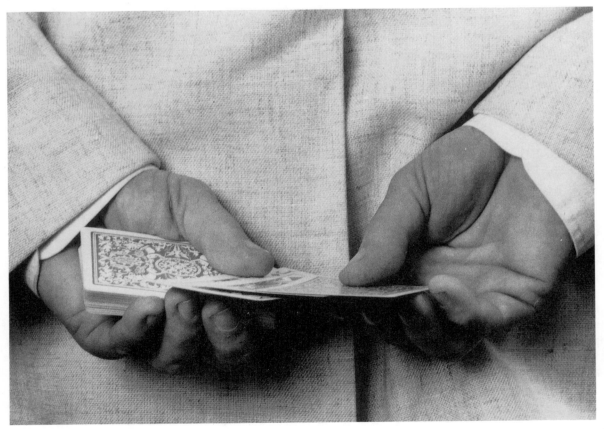

2

The Secret

If you run through this trick once you will see how easy it is to do. Openly remove the four aces, putting them face up on the table. Take the pack face down behind your back and explain that you are going to lose the aces in the pack in such a way that nobody, not even you, will know where they are. As you are talking, count off three cards from the top of the pack and turn them face up on the pack, then turn the top card over again. The order of the cards will now be, from the top down, one face-down card, two face-up cards, the rest of the pack face down. Now push the top three cards half across to the right of the pack and hold them against the pack with your left thumb **2**. In this position you will find it easy when you take the first ace from the table with your right hand to ostensibly insert it in the pack but actually to place it face up under the three cards you have partially separated from the rest of the pack **3**. The second ace is also placed face up under the three cards. The pack is now squared

up and the third ace is placed face down on top of the pack and the fourth ace also placed face down on top of it. The order of the cards from the top down will now be: face-down ace, face-down ace, face-down other card, two face-up other cards, face-up ace, face-up ace, the rest of the pack face down **4** (see p. 116).

Bring the pack out from behind your back, neatly squared, and ask the first spectator to cut off a small packet of about fourteen cards from the pack. Take the packet, turn it face up and place it square on top of the pack **5** (see p. 116). Spread through the face-up cards until you come to the first face-down one, remove the face-up cards as a packet and put them face up on the table **6** (see p. 117). Then deal the top card of the pack, which is face down, on top of the face-up packet on the table. You repeat this sequence three more times and then you are ready for the climax of the trick.

Important handling points to remember are that when you are spreading the face-up cards on the pack in your hands to reach a face-down

3

4 (see p. 115)

5 (see p. 115)

6 (see p. 115)

card (an ace), be careful not to spread the face-down cards in case you reveal the cards that are secretly hidden face up. At the end of the trick you will be left holding a small face-down packet of cards in which will be hidden two face-up cards. To clean up, just drop your hands below the table edge, find the face-up cards and turn them over so they are face down like the rest of the packet. If you do this while they are turning over their aces, no one will notice you casually drop your hands to your lap.

To work the trick smoothly, it is essential that you are able to handle the cards in a neat, controlled, unforced manner. To achieve that, like anything worthwhile, a little diligent practice is necessary. The trick is worth the effort.

GOOD EYE

Before you throw away that ancient, dog-eared pack of cards that has been lying around the house for ages, learn this super trick.

The Effect

The magician hands a pack of cards to a spectator and gets him to shuffle them thoroughly. He is told to select any card while you, the magician, turn your back. He then gives you the pack face down behind your back, which is held squared up. He is asked to insert his face-down selected card half-way into the pack **1** (see p. 118). You turn and face the spectator, still keeping the cards behind your

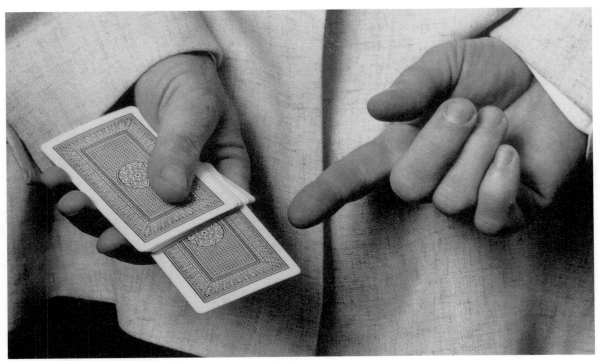

1 (see p. 117)

2 (see p. 119)

3

back. Ask him which is his good eye. Whichever he says it is, you look into it for a moment and announce the name of his selected card. You are seen to be correct when you bring the pack out from behind your back, as the selected card is still sticking half-way out of the pack.

The Secret

Presentation is everything in magic. It can cover a multitude of secrets – especially so in this trick, because, when the selected card has been returned to the pack behind your back and you turn to face the spectator, the business of asking him which is his good eye is really misdirection which completely diverts his attention from three secret moves in the following way.

'It's a medical fact that one eye is usually stronger than the other. Which is your good eye?' As you talk, you are facing the spectator. Behind your back you tear off the top left corner 2 of the selected card 3 and hold it in the curled second, third and fourth fingers of your right hand, so that the indice of the card is facing away from the fingers. Remember, the card was returned to the pack face down, so it's easy to keep track of the face of the card.

Whatever they say, bring your right hand out and point to their good eye with your forefinger, saying, 'So that is your good eye – the right one, not the left one, the right one.' Point to each eye in turn to match what you're saying. As you do this, glimpse the indice on the piece of card which is hidden in the curl of your fingers 4 (see p. 120). Don't make it obvious. Remember they have no idea what you are really up to.

4 (see p. 119)

5

'OK, I'm going to look deeply into your good eye for a moment. Yes, I can see it. Your card is the two of clubs.' As you're saying this, your right hand returns to the pack behind your back and turns the protruding selected card round in the pack by 180 degrees, so the torn half of the card is hidden in the pack. When you have announced the name of their card, bring the pack out from behind your back as con- firmation with your left hand. All they will see is their card sticking out of the pack exactly as they had placed it **5**. Push it flush into the pack and put the cards into your right pocket, thus disposing of the torn piece.

Your incentive to practise this trick until you can present it smoothly is the knowledge that it has badly fooled many well–informed magicians.

PERFECT POKER

The crooked gambler's ability to control the movement of cards during game play is the stuff of legend. Most people have heard of second and bottom deals, palmed cards, false shuffles, marked cards and loaded dice. It conjures up a Southern scene, with Mississippi paddle-steamers, gamblers in silk waistcoats and frilled cuffs with hidden pearl-handled Derringer pistols for instant use if challenged. The reality was, and is, very different.

For now, the following superb progressive poker deal will be sufficient to gain for you the appreciative response, 'I wouldn't like to play cards with you.'

The Effect
The magician offers to demonstrate how card-sharps control the cards during play. He divides the pack into three and gives each player a third of the pack to shuffle. He takes one third back, looks at the cards and rearranges them as he asks the other two players to look at their cards.

'Do you think as you look at your cards that you could influence the course of a game during successive deals?' he asks. 'Turn the cards face down in your hands. Now consider what you would have to do, and what would be involved, in tracking the position of every card and knowing exactly who has what in each hand. What sort of hands could you make from your cards. Very good players develop what is referred to as a card memory, which takes a lot of skill. I'll attempt to show you what I mean.'

The magician then deals four hands of poker. The first player to the dealer's left gets four tens and a jack. The second player gets two queens and three jacks. The third player gets two queens and three kings. The magician reveals his hand to be one king and four aces. He wins.

The magician gathers the cards up and deals again. Each player is dealt a royal flush. He gathers the cards and deals again. Each player is dealt a straight. He gathers the cards again and asks, 'What game am I demonstrating?'

The reply is poker. So he deals out four cards, in a row, spelling one card for each letter: P-O-K-E-R – and the card for R he places under those in his hand.

'What do we usually play for?' he asks. The reply is money. So he deals and spells one card for each letter on top of those on the table: M-O-N-E-Y – and the card for Y he places under those in his hand.

'And how do we win the money? We bet and raise the stakes by wagering.' He spells out W-A-G-E-R, a card being dealt and spelt for each letter and the card for R put under those in his hand.

'There are various types of poker. In our case we are playing draw poker.' He spells and deals one card for each letter of D-R-A-W. The fifth card he places under those in his hand.

'Now let's see what all that means,' he says as he turns over the four piles on the table. The first pile contains the four tens, the second the four jacks, the third the four queens and the fourth the four kings.

'Of course I get the four aces,' he declares, turning over the four cards in his hand.

The magician then gathers the cards up and instantly throws four packets of five cards on the table, one for each player. He turns them over to reveal that the first player has four tens and a jack, the second has three jacks and two queens, the third has two queens and three kings, and the magician has the winning hand, again: a king and four aces.

The Secret
Provided you follow the instructions to the letter, the trick works automatically.

Prior to performance remove the four tens, four jacks, four queens, four kings and the four aces from the pack. Shuffle them up and then put the packet face down on the table. On top of the packet place a joker. On top of the joker place the rest of the pack, including the second joker. Place the pack into the card case.

To present the trick, lead the conversation around to the game of poker. As the conversation progresses, casually pick up the card case and remove the pack. Spread the cards, faces towards yourself, as you look for the jokers. Separate the cards at the first joker and hand the packet, which contains the cards you had sorted earlier, to the person on your immediate left.

Find the second joker and place both jokers aside. Separate the remaining cards into two halves and hand them out for shuffling.

Take back the first packet from the person to your left and look at them as you patter about the difficulty of 'influencing' the game and 'card memory'.

Now we come to the one part of this book that will take real application – because, as you're talking, you have to sort through and stack the cards in your hand in the following order from left to right horizontally:

10C	JH	QS	KD	10H
JS	QD	AC	10S	JD
KC	AH	10D	QC	KH
AS	JC	QH	KS	AD

I've separated them into groups of five to help you memorize the order. When assembled in your hands the sequence will be the ten of clubs (10C) on top at the back through to the ace of diamonds (AD) on the front of the packet, as you look at them. When you turn the packet face down in a dealing position the ten of clubs will be on top.

I've suggested you commit the stack to memory, which is the ideal way to learn the method. Five minutes every day for a month is all you need to memorize the stack for ever. It's worth the application.

If, however, you prefer an easier method, all you need to do is to write the stack order lightly in pencil on the face of the joker that you use to separate your pre-stacked cards from the rest of the pack. When you sort through the cards looking for the jokers, keep this one on top of your packet of cards when you separate them from the rest of the pack, then divide the remaining cards into two halves and hand the cards out for shuffling.

When you take your packet back, locate the joker and put it on the face of your packet. While you're talking, rearrange the cards into the stacked sequence. Remember you are apparently sorting through the cards to see what hands are possible as you talk, so don't be too self-conscious about it. Do it casually and say things like 'Hm, there might be something here' and 'How about you, anything?' Bear in mind they don't know what you are going to do. And with practice you will be able to assemble the stack very quickly.

When you are ready, flash the face of the joker as you discard it and leave it face down on the table.

Your first deal, starting with the person on your left, will reveal the following cards:

Hand 1 – four tens and a jack
Hand 2 – three jacks and two queens
Hand 3 – two queens and three kings
Hand 4 – (the magician's hand) a king and four aces.

Don't disturb the order of the cards as you turn them over and display them.

Pick up hand 1 and hold it face down in your left hand. On top of it place hand 2, then hand 3 and, finally, hand 4, the magician's hand.

Now deal four hands again and reveal that each hand is a royal flush. Pick up the cards as before in hand 1, 2, 3, 4 sequence.

Deal another four hands and reveal that each hand now contains a straight. As the cards in each hand won't be in ten to ace order, you must rearrange them. It is perfectly natural to do this, because you are showing that each hand is a straight, so you arrange the cards to show exactly that. The cards in each hand will then be in ten, jack, queen, king, ace order. The tens will be at the bottom of each face-up hand, the aces on the face.

Pick up each hand, in order now, and hold the cards face down in your left hand. Now deal one card for each letter of P-O-K-E in a row from left to right, the card for the final R going under the packet in your hand.

Deal another card along the row for each letter you spell of M-O-N-E on top of those on the table. The card for the final Y goes underneath those in your hand.

Then deal another card along the row for each letter you spell of W-A-G-E-R on top of those on the table. The card for the last letter R goes underneath those in your hand.

Finally spell and deal one card for each letter of D-R-A-W on to the four piles on the table. The cards in your hand, which we will call the fifth pile, you put near you to one side.

Turn over each pile on the table, starting with the first pile. This will reveal the four tens. The second pile will contain the four jacks, the third the four queens, the fourth the four kings. And the last pile, which is my pile invariably, contains the four aces.

At this point the trick seems to be over, so scant attention will be paid to the fact that you gather up the fifth pile (the aces) and put it face down into your left hand, followed by the fourth pile, the third pile, the second and the first.

Now very quickly count and push over five cards into your right hand and drop them in front of the first player to your left. Push off five more cards and drop them in front of the second player. Push off another five cards and drop them in front of the third player. And drop the remaining five on the table in front of yourself. Try to do all this very casually.

'It's interesting, isn't it?' you remark. 'Turn over the cards in your hands.' Then reveal the cards in your hand as you say, 'I win again. Now you know why good gamblers don't gamble.'

Although this has taken some describing, some genuine practice will prove that there is nothing difficult in the routine. Just try practising with the cards in hand and you'll see how straightforward it is. Memorizing the stack, if you choose to, and casually sorting the cards into stack sequence are the elements to concentrate on. Not everybody will put in the effort. Those who do will have a marvellous effect at their fingertips.

THE MASTER CARDMAN

This truly amazing demonstration is one of the 'plums' of this book. Three outstanding tricks are combined to create a routine that will impress, entertain, intrigue and baffle the keenest of card players. If any series of tricks in the whole of magic warranted the time spent in practice, these are the ones.

The Effect
The magician shuffles and cuts a borrowed pack of cards. He has four cards selected and placed sight unseen on the table in front of each spectator. Each person is then given approximately a quarter of the pack to shuffle. (The cards are genuinely mixed.)

The magician states that he will turn his back and use his phenomenal card memory to find the selected cards. He will achieve this by calling every card in the pack, in a random order, never naming the same card twice. As each card is called, it is to be placed face up on top of the preceding cards in a pile on the table.

And this is exactly what he does. He calls forty-eight cards in succession. At which point he turns and faces the four spectators, each of whom is left with a single card. The magician states that he believes that each of these are the original selected cards. He then tells each spectator in turn the name of the card face down in front of them. They confirm he is correct. Gathering up all the cards, he mixes them again with a series of fast cuts and asks if any of the spectators play bridge. He tells them that people generally have a mistaken concept of what a card cheat is and what he does. As he talks, the magician deals out four hands of bridge, explaining that people have a clichéd image of a card cheat. They imagine him to be someone who dresses flamboyantly, exhibits fabulous skills and rakes in enormous amounts of money from gullible gamblers. In fact, nothing could be further from the truth. The card cheat's greatest skill is in hiding his skill, for if he is suspected, even for a moment, he is finished. 'Would you believe,' he asks, 'that as I have been talking and dealing the cards I've been using my skills to cheat? Look, I'll show you.'

With this he turns the cards over and reveals the first three hands he dealt and explains that, although you could compile a reasonable hand out of each, there would be no point because he has dealt himself the perfect winning bridge hand in spades. He reveals his own hand to prove this.

Next he gathers up the cards and gives them another series of rapid cuts. He then proceeds to deal five hands of poker, explaining as he does so that the card cheat's real objective is not to win one spectacular jackpot but continuously to manipulate the cards to create an advantage in play situation – the advantage being to himself. And it is this 'edge' that enables him to win steadily on a continuous basis, rather than to go for the one big 'hit' that would excite suspicion.

For example, he continues, whilst I have been dealing I have built up the hands in the following way. To the first player on my left I dealt three twos. The next I gave only a pair of jacks. The third player two fours and a pair of kings, not a bad hand. The fourth player got just a pair of tens. To myself I dealt a poor hand, although I have an ace. He has revealed the contents of each hand as he has spoken.

He continues by telling the spectators that by dealing these cards in actual play each player would be encouraged by his hand to continue and not fold, therefore putting more money into the pot. 'Let's see how the game progresses.'

The first player would discard and draw two cards. He deals two cards face down next to the three face-up twos, removing the other two.

The second player would call for three cards, hoping to improve his hand. He deals three cards next to the two face-up jacks, removing the other three discards.

The third player discarded his pair of fours and his odd card, retaining his pair of kings and calling for three cards, which are dealt face down next to the kings.

The fourth player kept his pair of tens, discarded three and drew three, which are dealt face down next to the tens.

The magician had little choice but to retain his single ace, discard the other four and take four, which are dealt face down next to his ace. Now, he explains, after looking at their hands, each player would fancy their chances and bet heavily on the outcome. And so it was time to show their hands.

The first player, even with three twos, hadn't improved his hand at all. The second player had got a pair of queens, giving him a reasonable hand – jacks and queens. The third player, who was proving to be a canny gambler, had drawn three eights, giving him a full house. The fourth player made three tens. But none of them stood a chance, because the card cheat had dealt himself the other three aces to win all the money in the pot.

And the thing is, nobody suspected a thing.

The Secret
The first point to emphasize about this routine is that there is nothing difficult in it. You can do it. The key to acquiring facility with it is to practise.

So what does it consist of? A bold force of four cards and, ideally, the memorization of fifty-two cards. Or, as a substitute, the subtle, unobtrusive use of a gimmick to enable you to call the entire pack apparently from memory. Plus a very deceptive gambler's false cut and false shuffle. The main requirement is a confident presentation.

Start with the pack in its card case. It doesn't matter what order the cards are in as long as you have the following four cards on top of the pack, in the following order: on top, the two of hearts, second, the four of diamonds, third, the nine of hearts and, fourth, the ace of spades. The jokers can be anywhere in the pack.

In your pocket you have a piece of card, small enough to palm in your hand, used in much the same way as the gimmick in the 'Knight's Tour' described in Chapter 2. On the piece of card are listed the following cards, which are read vertically column by column.

1.	6H	14.	4H
2.	3C	15.	10C
3.	AH	16.	6S
4.	QS	17.	5C
5.	3H	18.	JD
6.	7D	19.	KC
7.	QC	20.	10S
8.	7S	21.	4C
9.	2C	22.	2D
10.	10D	23.	JC
11.	AC	24.	4S
12.	JS	25.	7H
13.	5D	26.	6D
27.	8H	40.	9S
28.	2S	41.	KD
29.	7C	42.	5H
30.	9D	43.	3D
31.	8C	44.	5S
32.	KS	45.	JH
33.	AD	46.	9C
34.	KH	47.	QD
35.	8D	48.	8S
36.	3S	49.	2H
37.	10H	50.	4D
38.	6C	51.	9H
39.	QH	52.	AS

To present the effect, take the pack from its case and run through the cards to remove the jokers. False shuffle, retaining the top stock (your set-up of four cards) (see pages 89–90). Then false cut in the hands, page 95.

Deal one card, face down on the table. In this way you have forced four cards, in a known order, to each spectator. So the first spectator, on your left, will have received the two of hearts and the fourth spectator, on your right, will have received the ace of spades, although they aren't aware of this yet.

Next you cut the pack into four approximately equal packets and give them to each of the assisting spectators with the request that they shuffle them thoroughly. You then turn and walk away from the card table and stand with your back to them. You will want to be of a sufficient distance from the table so that as far as the spectators are concerned you obviously can't see or influence what they are doing. In fact, you have walked away for another reason: you don't want them to see what you are really doing, which is reading the cards from the small card palmed in your hand.

Let's look at the exact sequence of moves. You have given them four packets of cards to shuffle. You explain that you are going to stand facing away from the table so there is no possibility of your seeing any of the cards. Make gestures with your hands as you talk so that subliminally they register the fact you have nothing in your hands, and also clench your hands together in front of your body. Then you can casually put your hands in your pockets as you ask them if they understand your instructions – that as you call out the name of each card they are to sort through their packets and, whoever locates it, is to place it face up on the table; the next card called will be placed face up on top of that and so on.

Palm the piece of card in your hand as you are talking, then, when you turn and walk away, take your hands from your pockets and clench them together in front of your body. Tell them that of course everybody knows all the cards in the pack and could call them out in ace to king suit order, but you have memorized the cards in a totally random order and will attempt to call every card in the pack without repetition. What you simply do is call out the cards in the listed order. It should be obvious to you that you don't recite the cards as though you were reading from a list! You must

sometimes hesitate and there will be moments of confidence where you name four or five cards in quick succession. Your body language is important. Your head should look up and down and sideways as though you are concentrating fiercely to recall the cards from memory. You must make expressive gestures with your hands (obviously keeping the gimmick unseen by switching it from hand to hand) and arms. The important thing to convey is the difficulty of the feat.

Progress through the listed cards and when you reach number 48, the eight of spades, dump the gimmick into your pocket as you reach in for a handkerchief to mop your brow as you turn and walk to the table naming the card.

'There are four cards left on the table,' you continue. 'Having heard forty-eight cards called, without repetition, do you think with your card memories you could name any of these cards?'

The answer will be no. Turn to the spectator on your left and say, 'Your card is the two of hearts.' Turn it over to prove it and put it face up on the pile of cards on the table.

To the second you say, 'Your card is the four of diamonds.' Turn it over and place it face up on the pile. To the third, 'Your card, and it's the fifty-first card I am calling from memory, is the nine of hearts.' Turn it over and put it with the others.

To the last spectator you say, 'Wouldn't it be awful if I got your card wrong? I will tell you that there is a story connected with your card. A Corsican witch once brewed a mysterious potion which helped her to foresee the future of Napoleon Bonaparte. The ingredients in this concoction were two adders, twenty-four spiders, seven toads, a ewe lamb's heart and the ace of spades.' Turn the card and add it to the face-up pile on the table.

As you are taking your applause, false cut the cards in your hand several times using the gambler's false cut. Now go into your bridge deal as you talk about card cheats. By dealing quickly and rhythmically you will be able to complete the deal to synchronize with your patter. Reveal the faces of each hand, beginning with the first spectator's cards. You have dealt yourself a winning bridge hand.

Pick up each hand as a packet in reverse order, starting with the spades, and reassemble the pack. False cut the cards again and deal five hands of poker, four of which are dealt singly from left to right across the table. You are now demonstrating a poker deal, so you are not dealing to the assisting spectators. The layout is four hands across the table; the fifth – which is your hand – is dealt in front of you. Turn over each hand as you talk, rearranging the cards to illustrate your patter and to make it easy to pick up the discards later. Run off the appropriate number of cards to replace the discards in each hand and reveal each new hand in turn, as described earlier, until you reach your knock-out climax.

This routine has taken a lot of describing to teach you the essential details that make the difference between guesswork and certainty when practising. Learn the routine thoroughly so that you can do it without reference to the text, then think about your presentation and patter and how you will handle the gimmick. Is there a better way? For example, it could be stuck on the back of the wide end of your tie, so when your back is towards the spectators you can simply turn the tie over and your hands need never go to your pockets. But which way up should you stick the gimmick? What is the best way? I'll let you solve that. Because when you think about it, you will be thinking like a magician. When you start thinking like a magician, you're on your way to becoming one. Persevere and you will make it.

CHAPTER 10
CARD NOVELTIES

The race is not always to the swift, nor the battle to the strong, but that's the way to bet. – *Damon Runyon*

This chapter contains a little of the lighter side of card conjuring. Mix these in with your miracles and nobody will nod off. In this section you will find not tricks, but oddities and novelties that can be demonstrated with a pack of cards. These somewhat esoteric stunts are intriguing enough to qualify as entertainment, for they will certainly engage the interest of your spectators, particularly those who regularly play cards.

SPELLING THE PACK

One way of checking that you have a full pack of fifty-two cards (minus jokers) prior to play, or performance, is to count them. Another more interesting way is to spell them. Simply deal one card for each letter of each card from A-C-E through to K-I-N-G. So you would deal A-C-E, then T-W-O, followed by T-H-R-E-E, then F-O-U-R, dealing one card for each letter, F-I-V-E, then S-I-X, etc. You will find that the fifty-second card dealt will fall on the G of K-I-N-G.

If you find this oddity curious, you will definitely appreciate that it gets curiouser and curiouser when I tell you that it also works in Swedish, Dutch and French and even in German, allowing for the fact that the 'ch' in 'sechs' and 'acht' is articulated, and counted, as one letter.

ODD COUPLES

It was the contention of Robert Harbin, one of the truly inventive magicians, that more often than not in a thoroughly shuffled pack a king and a three will be found together [1] (see p. 128). And, curiously, over the years, whenever I have shuffled a pack of cards I have found this invariably to be the case – strange but true. Try it for yourself right now. If you decide to

English		Swedish		Dutch		French		German	
ace	3	ess	3	ass	3	as	2	as	2
two	3	tvan	4	twee	4	deux	4	zwei	4
three	5	trea	4	drie	4	trois	5	drei	4
four	4	fyra	4	veir	4	quatre	6	vier	4
five	4	femma	5	vyf	3	cinq	4	funf	4
six	3	sexa	4	zes	3	six	3	sechs	4
seven	5	ajua	4	zeven	5	sept	4	sieben	6
eight	5	atta	4	acht	4	huit	4	acht	3
nine	4	nia	3	negen	5	neuf	4	neun	4
ten	3	tia	3	tien	4	dix	3	zehn	4
jack	4	knekt	5	boer	4	valet	5	bube	4
queen	5	dam	3	vrouw	5	reine	5	dame	4
king	4	kung	6	heer	4	roi	3	donig	5
	—		—		—		—		—
	52		52		52		52		52

Spelling the Pack

1 (see p. 127)

show this to your audience, present it as a mini-prediction. Get someone to shuffle the cards and say casually, 'I may be wrong, but I get a distinct feeling that somewhere in the pack you will find a king and a three next to each other.' If this is verified, it's a nice quickie. If not, say, 'Maybe later.' And later on try it again. The probability is that it will work.

WIND-UP

Here's an amusing bit of business. Hold a pack of cards in your left hand in a dealing position, then curl your forefinger in and underneath the pack so that the first phalange, the length of the nail on the top of the finger to the first joint, is

1 Wind-Up

pressed against the pack. Now take your thumb off the cards and you will be able to grip the cards firmly between the fleshy base of the thumb and your second, third and fourth fingers. In this position you will be able to riffle the outer top-left corner of the pack briskly with your left thumb, producing a short, sharp, zipping sound **1**. The gag is to pretend to wind up the pack by turning an imaginary key against the back of the top card of the pack with your right hand, each turn of the key synchronizing with a riffle of the pack **2**. It's a nice start to some card tricks or an effective 'get-out joke' if something goes wrong.

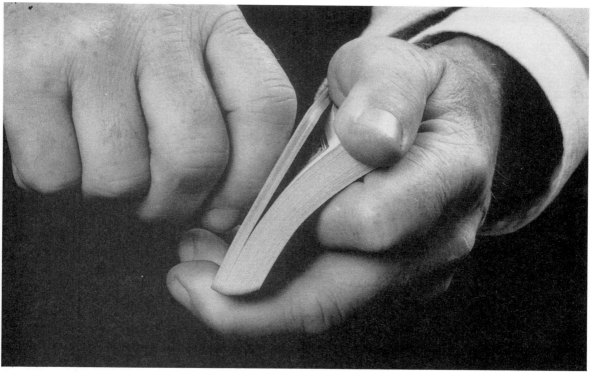

2

CHECKING THE PACK

Another gag using the same riffling sound effect is to pretend to count the number of cards in the pack in a split second.

Set up the pack so that there is a joker on the face and a joker in the middle. Remove the pack from its case, remove the visible joker and put it aside as you say, 'We don't use the joker. So now I've got a full fifty-two-card pack.' Pause. Raise the pack to your left ear – you can use both hands to hold the pack if you find it easier – and listen intently as you riffle the pack briskly with your left thumb tip **1**. Say, 'Just a minute. That doesn't sound right.' Sort

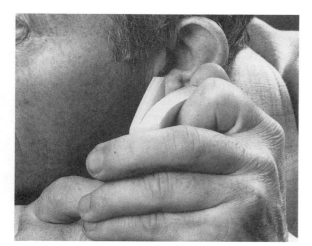

1 (Checking the Pack)

through the pack and remove the other joker.

Done casually, as though you really are checking the number of cards in the pack, it's a nice offbeat gag that will amuse people.

TURN-UP

Deal the following thirteen cards, irrespective of suits, face down in a pile on the table, starting with a ten, then a six, king, five, nine, four, jack, three, eight, two, queen, ace and finally a seven on top. Hold the cards face down in your left hand in dealing position, take the top card and place it face down underneath the packet. Deal the next card face up on the table. The next goes face down under the packet and the next you deal face up on to the card on the table. The next one goes under the packet, then one face up on top of the cards on the table, and so on until you have dealt all the cards. You will end up with a line of cards in ace through to king sequence, having left the indices exposed.

This little puzzle will appeal particularly to bridge players, who may try to reconstruct what happened. But unless you show them the stack – and you won't will you? – they will have great difficulty making it work.

CARD-PLAYERS' QUIZ

How well do you know the cards in the pack? For people who handle cards a lot, whether playing games like bridge or poker or even doing card tricks, here is a very testing little card quiz which is perfect to introduce at the card table.

Jacks
1. How many 'one-eyed' jacks are there?
2. What is the predominant colour of the hat each jack wears?
3. What are the colours of the patterned line work on each jack's hat and which is ascribed to whom?
4. Which jack has the most curls in his hair?
5. How many jacks face left?
6. How many jacks have a moustache?

Queens
1. What do all the queens hold in their hands?
2. How many queens face to the right?

Kings
1. How many kings wear a beard?
2. How many kings have four hands showing?
3. How many kings hold an axe?
4. How many kings hold a sword?
5. How many kings hold a sword upright?
6. How many kings have a moustache?
7. How many kings face left?

If you play this card quiz with a few people, you can easily determine the winner by having them jot their answers down on paper. Come to think of it, how many questions did you answer correctly without reference to the pack?

DROP CHALLENGE

Take five cards and stand over an empty hat or a small waste-paper basket placed mouth up on the floor, and drop one card at a time into it. You should drop them from about chest height. You can take your time and line each card up as carefully as you like before dropping it. How many cards out of five did you successfully drop into the container?

The answer is likely to be none, because you didn't know the correct method of dropping the cards. You probably held each card vertically by its short top edge **1**. This almost always guarantees failure. What guarantees success is to hold each card horizontally in relation to the floor with your thumb at one short edge and your fingers at the other **2**. Sight the card over the hat and drop it. Bingo! **3**

You can have a lot of fun with your card-table partners with this trick. Present it as a challenge. Whether you choose to show them the correct method of holding and dropping the cards is a matter of choice. If you feel they will have more fun trying to do it again another day, then keep the secret to yourself.

1

2

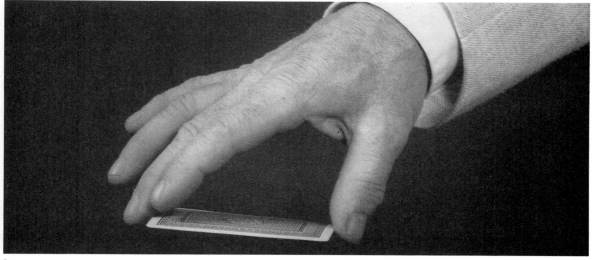

3

TURN-UP CHALLENGE

Here is a very good little card puzzle which is just perfect for bridge players. Deal three cards face down in a row on the table in front of each participant. We'll assume there are four players. Make them each turn the centre card of their row of three face up. This is the start position. The challenge is to finish with all three cards face up, in three (not two) moves only, turning over two cards per move. (The solution is given at the end of this chapter.)

The simplicity of this puzzle is actually the reason that some people struggle. Mentally they complicate the puzzle and confuse themselves out of a solution. For those who do solve it easily, offer the next puzzle.

THE THINKING CARD-PLAYER'S PUZZLE

You place three cards face down in a row on the table and state, 'This puzzle is solved by decoding the following information. We will mentally number the cards one, two and three, reading from left to right. Now listen carefully. There is at least one three to the right of a two – which means that the card at number two, or the card at number three, must be a three There is at least one three just to the left of a three. There is at least one club just to the left of a diamond. There is at least one club just to the right of a club. The thinking card-player's puzzle is to name the three cards. Good luck.'

This will take a little solving, but good card-players, and good thinkers, should be able to do it and will be pleasantly amused. We have given the solution at the end of this chapter so that you can amuse yourself with it before confirming your own solution.

THE PERPETUAL ALMANACK OR GENTLEMAN'S PRAYER BOOK

Showing how one Richard Middleton was taken before the Mayor of the City he was in, for using cards in Church during Divine Service; being a droll, merry, and humorous account of an odd affair that happened to a private soldier in the 6th Regiment of Foot.

This was the introduction to a broadsheet describing the curious event in a day in the life of Richard Middleton, which circulated in England during the early part of Queen Victoria's reign. But certainly 'The Devil's Tickets', 'The Soldier's Bible' or 'The Deck of Cards Story' was a lot older than that. Its origins can be traced back over three hundred years. Variations on it have developed through war and peace, the story and church setting being adapted by successive popularizers to Napoleonic encounters, Civil War legends, First World War attrition and Second World War blitzkreig. Its most recent incarnations have seen a now nameless Richard Middleton transported to the North African campaign and to the top of most of the world's pop-charts by an American country and western singer. You can't keep a good story down. And this is a good story.

The sergeant commanded his party to the church, and when the parson had ended his prayer, he took his text; and all them that had a Bible pulled it out to find the text, but this soldier had neither Bible, Almanack, nor Common Prayer book; but he put his hand in his pocket and pulled out a pack of cards, and spread them before him as he sat. While the parson was preaching, he first kept looking at one card and then at another. The sergeant of the company saw him, and said, 'Richard, put up your cards; for this is no place for them.' 'Never mind that,' said the

A Magician at Prayer

soldier, 'for you have no business with me here.'

When the parson had ended his sermon, and all was over, the soldiers repaired to the churchyard, and the commanding officer gave the word of command to fall in, which they did. The sergeant of the city came and took the man prisoner. 'Man, you are my prisoner,' said he. 'Sir' said the soldier, 'What have I done that I am your prisoner?' 'You have played a game of cards in the church.' 'No,' said the soldier, 'I have not play'd a game, for I only look'd at a pack.' 'No matter for that, you are my prisoner.' 'Where must we go?' said the soldier. 'You must go before the mayor,' said the sergeant.

So he took him before the mayor; and when they came to the mayor's house he was at dinner. When he had dined, he came to them and said, 'Well, sergeant, what do you want with me?' 'I have brought a soldier before your honour, for playing cards in the church.' 'What! That soldier.' 'Yes.' 'Well, soldier, what have you to say for yourself?' 'Much, sir, I hope.' 'Well and good, but if you have not you shall be punished the worst that ever man was.' 'Sir,' said the soldier, 'I have been five weeks upon the march, and have but little to subsist on, and am without either Bible, Almanack, or Common Prayer book, or anything but a pack of cards. I hope to satisfy your honour of the purity of my intention.'

Then the soldier pulled out of his pocket the pack of cards, which he spread before the mayor, and then began with the ace.

'When I see the ace,' said he, 'it puts me in mind that there is one God only; and when I see the deuce, it puts me in mind of the Father and the Son; when I see the tray, it puts me in mind of the Father, Son and the Holy Ghost; when I see the four it puts me in mind of the four Evangelists that preached the gospel, viz., Matthew, Mark, Luke, and John; when I see the five it puts me in mind of the five wise virgins that trimmed their lamps; there were ten, but five were foolish, who were shut out; when I see the six, it puts me in mind that in six days the Lord made Heaven and Earth; when I see the seven, it puts me in mind that the seventh day God rested from all the works which he had created and made, wherefore the Lord blessed the seventh day and hallowed it; when I see the eight, it puts me in mind of the eight righteous persons that were saved when God drowned the world, viz., Noah, his wife, three sons, and their wives; when I see the nine, it puts me in mind of nine lepers that were cleansed by our Saviour, there were ten, but nine never returned God thanks; when I see the ten, it puts me in mind of the ten commandments that God gave Moses on Mount Sinai on the two tablets of stone.'

Here he took the knave and laid it aside.

'When I see the queen, it puts me in mind of the Queen of Sheba, who came from the furthermost parts of the world to hear the wisdom of King Solomon, and who was as wise a woman as he was a man; for she brought fifty boys and fifty girls, all clothed in boys' apparel, to show before King Solomon, for him to tell which were boys and which were girls; but he could not until he called for water for them to wash themselves; the girls washed up to their elbows, and the boys only up to their wrists, so King Solomon told by that. And also of Queen Victoria – the queen of our hearts – to pray for her. And when I see the King, it put me in mind of the great King of Heaven and Earth, which is God Almighty.'

'Well,' said the mayor, 'you have given a very good description of all the cards except one, which is lacking.' 'Which is that?' said the soldier. 'The knave,' said the mayor. 'Oh, I can give your honour a good description of that, if your honour won't be angry.' 'No, I will not,' says the mayor, 'if you will not term me the knave.'

'Well,' said the soldier, 'the greatest fool that I know of is the sergeant of the city that brought me here.' 'I don't know,' said the mayor, 'that he is the greatest knave, but I am sure he is the greatest fool.'

'I shall now show your honour how I use the cards as an Almanack.' 'You certainly are a clever fellow,' said the mayor, 'but I think you will have a hard matter to make that appear.'

'When I count how many spots there are

in a pack of cards, I find there are three hundred and sixty-five, there are so many days in the year.'

'Stop,' said the mayor, 'that's a mistake.' 'I grant it,' said the soldier, 'but as I have never yet seen an almanack that was thoroughly correct in all points it would have been impossible for me to imitate an almanack exactly, without a mistake.' 'Your observations are very correct,' said the mayor; 'go on.' 'When I count how many cards there are in a pack, I find there are fifty-two; there are so many weeks in the year; there are four suits in the pack which represent the four seasons of the year. You see, sir, that this pack of cards is a Bible, Almanack, Common Prayer book, and Pack of Cards to me.'

Then the mayor called for a loaf of bread, a piece of cheese, and a pot of good beer, and gave to the soldier a piece of money, bidding him to go about his business, saying he was the cleverest man he had ever seen.

The Set-up and Effect

The story lends itself naturally to demonstration. Here is the stack and the bare bones of the story, plus a red, black, day and night addition which is easily incorporated, as is the joker variant.

Sort the pack into the four suits and arrange each suit in ace to king sequence. From the top of the pack down stack the cards in the following order **1**:

Ace to king of hearts and the joker – face down
Ace to king of diamonds – face up
Ace to king of clubs – face up
Ace to king of spades – face up.

As you tell the story, you turn up each appropriate card and lay them down progressively from your right to left **2** (see p. 136).

The first part of the story is purely narrative. 'The sergeant commands his party to the church, and when . . .' to 'Then the soldier pulled out of his pocket the pack of cards . . .' *Take the pack from the card case and hold the cards face down in a dealing position.*
Ace – 'one God'. *Lay the ace of hearts to the right of the centre of the table.*
Two – 'The Old and New Testaments'. *Place it next to the ace.*

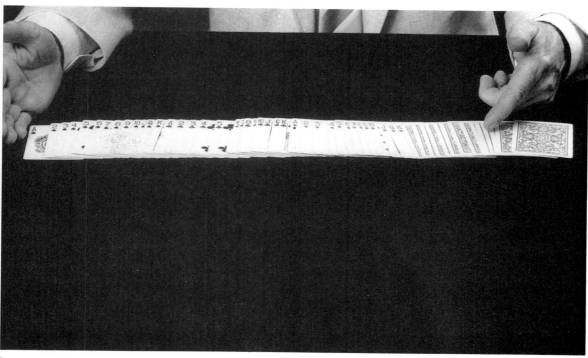

1

2 (see p. 135)

Three – 'Father, Son and the Holy Ghost'. *Place it next to the two.*

Four – 'Matthew, Mark, Luke, and John'. *Place it next to the three.*

The rest of the cards follow this layout.

Five – 'the five wise virgins'.

Six – 'in six days the Lord made Heaven and Earth'.

Seven – 'the seventh day God rested'.

Eight – 'the eight righteous persons that were saved . . . Noah, his wife, three sons, and their wives'.

Nine – 'nine lepers'.

Ten – 'the ten commandments'.

Jack – 'the knave', the sergeant as in the story or it can be a reminder of the Devil and his temptations.

Queen – 'the Queen of Sheba'.

King – 'The King of Heaven and Earth'.

The position now is that the ace of hearts are laid out face up in a line from your right to left, starting to the right of the centre of the table. Now put the rest of the pack on the table above the ace of hearts nearest to you and make a long face up ribbon spread across the table as you say **3**, 'When I count how many spots there are in a pack of cards . . .' This makes a nice display for the closing part of the story.

Additional Points

You can employ the joker as the 365th day of a leap year, turning it face up and counting it as one spot **4**.

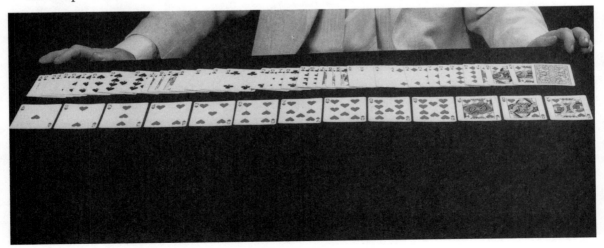

3

A diary confirms the almanack

If you are challenged about the actual number of spot cards, point out that by spots we mean numerical values, counting eleven for the jack, twelve for the queen and thirteen for the king.

For clarity, you may decide to insert the words 'also' and 'thirteen' into the line 'there are so many lunar months in the year'.

You can also use the joker, holding it to point with when adding that the red and black division of colour represents the red of the sun for day and black for the dark of night as part of the Almanack description.

Although most people are vaguely aware of the story, very few have ever seen it performed with pack in hand. The sequence is easily remembered, each card acting as a visual memory aid. For the little time and minimal trouble involved in preparing the set-up, you will be rewarded with a perfect party piece.

4

SOLUTIONS

Turn-up Challenge

Reading from left to right, mentally number the cards 1, 2 and 3. The start condition and three moves required to resolve this puzzle are as follows:

Start: Card 1 face down
             Card 2 face up
             Card 3 face down
Move 1:   Turn over cards 2 and 3
Move 2:   Turn over cards 1 and 3
Move 3:   Turn over cards 2 and 3

An even simpler solution is to turn over cards 1 and 3 consecutively three times. Simple though this is some people will struggle. For those who don't, use it as a come-on for the next trick.

The Thinking Card-Player's Puzzle

The three cards are the two of clubs, the three of clubs and the three of diamonds.

The deductive logic that you have applied to solve this puzzle will have gone along these Sherlockian lines:

There is at least one three just to the right of a two. Therefore it stands to reason that either the card at number 2 or the card at number 3 is a three, as both are the only cards to the right of another card. There is at least one three just to the left of a three. Therefore it stands to reason that either the card at number 1 or the card at number 2 is a three. And as card number 2 has twice been identified as a three, it *must* be a three. And as we also know that there is a three just to the right of a two, logic dictates that card number 1 is a two. And as we know that there is a three (card number 1) just to the left of a three, we can determine that card number 3 is a three. The disposition of the suits is determined by the same reasoning process.

CHAPTER 11
SIX GREAT CARD TRICKS

The two leading recipes for success are building a better mousetrap and finding a bigger loophole. – *Edgar A. Shoaff*

Although this is not the longest chapter in the book, it contains six of the very best tricks. One word of advice: don't attempt to perform all these together. Each is a 'closer', with the exception of 'Dial a Miracle', which has a unique presentation. These are very strong performance tricks that will baffle the keenest brains and, indeed, have fooled many magicians in their time! Practise them well and you will be rewarded many times over by the response of your spectators.

COMPULSION

Here is a miraculous effect in which the method and presentation cunningly combine to misdirect the spectator away from any conceivable explanation of the mystery.

The Effect
The magician should present this trick with the rather lofty delivery of an after-dinner speaker along the following lines.

'Ladies and gentlemen, I should like to give a brief dissertation on the subject and theme of compulsion. *Webster's Dictionary* defines compulsion as "an act of compelling, the state of being compelled". A further definition is: "a force or agency that compels". And finally, "an irresistible impulse to perform an irrational act". An irresistible impulse. A force or agency that compels. Sounds a little spooky. Well, let's test the validity of those definitions.

'Sir, you look like a man who, to my trained magician's eye, can shuffle a pack of cards. Yes, of course you can. Please take this pack of cards, remove them from their case and shuffle them as many times as you like. I shall turn away. Have you finished? Good. Hold the cards face down in your left hand. I shall now face you. I have a question for you. Do you think it is possible that anybody in this room, or on this planet, could conceivably know the order, the positions of the cards in relation to each other in the shuffled pack you are holding? You don't think it's possible? Neither do I. Well, having established that, I would like you to begin dealing the cards one at a time in a pile on the table. Before you start, let me show you this. As you can see, I have taken from my pocket an envelope, and written on the envelope is this word again – compulsion. I shall place it here on the edge of the table within your range of vision. Now please begin dealing the cards on the table. Don't worry about the pile – it doesn't have to be particularly neat. That's fine. As you're dealing I want you to stop any time you feel like it. Where you stop is totally up to you, and I shall stop talking while you're dealing in case you feel I may influence you in some way.

'There? You wish to stop there? You may change your mind if you wish. You can continue dealing and stop again if you want to. It's your choice. No? You'll stop where you are. OK. Now I'll pick up the envelope by my fingertips and draw your attention to this powerful word "compulsion". I'll drop it in front of you. Were you conscious of that word while you were dealing? Yes? No? Well, there is more to this envelope than you know. Pick it up and turn it over. Immediately you'll notice two things. One, that it is sealed. And two, that written across the sealed flap is "10.31 p.m., 26 March". That's yesterday's date, and at that exact time yesterday I felt compelled to seal something in the envelope you're holding. Please open it, take out what's inside and hold it

up for all to see. It is a single playing-card, from a different pack, the three of clubs. Sir, please turn over the last card you dealt on to the table. It is also the three of clubs.

'Thank you for your applause. Before we finish, may I ask you, sir, what made you stop dealing when you did? Were you exercising freedom of choice? Was it a coincidence? Were you compelled to stop? Was there some strange force or agency at work? Is it possible it was an act of *compulsion*?'

The Secret

The preamble and style of presentation is intended subtly to divert the audience's attention away from the very simple and quite bold ploy that makes the trick work. A word of caution: don't think less of this trick because of its simplicity. Rather, admire its marvellous economy of method. Such simplicity is the means behind many of the most wonderful effects in magic, whether small close-up tricks or full-size stage illusions.

To prepare for the trick take a playing-card – our example is the three of clubs – from another pack. Seal it inside an opaque envelope, then write over the sealed flap a time and date that precedes the day of performance. On the front of the envelope write the word 'compulsion' in capital letters and place the envelope face down on the table, so the flap side is up. Now take the pack of cards that the spectator will use in the performance and remove the three of clubs from the pack. Place it face up on the envelope. Now pick up the card and the envelope together and practise passing them from hand to hand so that the card remains hidden behind the envelope. Anybody facing you would see you holding an envelope with the word 'compulsion' written on it and would have no reason to suspect that you are secretly concealing a playing-card behind the envelope **1**. Now practise placing the card and envelope on a table, so that they overlap the table edge sufficiently to enable you to pick up the card and envelope easily and cleanly without fumbling, and so that there is no risk of either the card or envelope falling off the table. It will

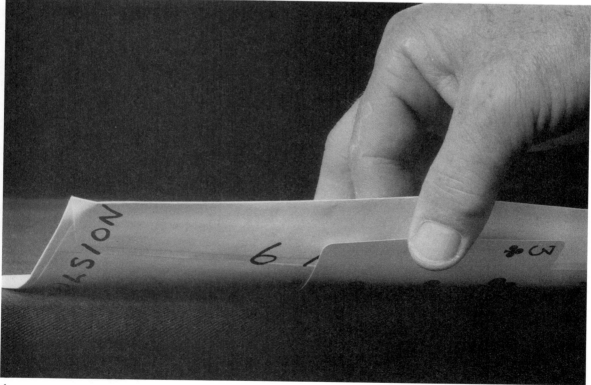

1

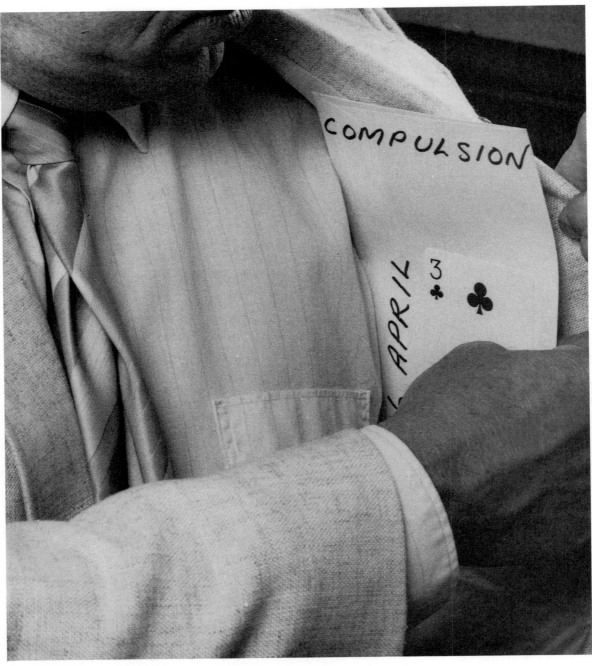

2

become apparent to you that your thumb will always hold the card against the envelope and that your fingertips will be against the front of the envelope. Now place the card and envelope inside your jacket pocket so that the three of clubs facing towards your body **2**. Practise taking the card and envelope from your pocket **3**, keeping the card hidden at all times. Don't be too self-conscious about what you are doing. Just handle them with a nice light touch exactly as you would ordinarily handle an envelope. Finally, practise dropping the envelope face up

3

on top of the pile of cards dealt on to the table **4** (see p. 144). The word 'compulsion' will be facing your assistant from the audience. To the spectators it will appear that you have casually dropped the envelope in front of your assistant for him to pick up.

What you have really done is to add the hidden three of clubs on top of the pile of cards on the table.

Practise this move until you can do it with the necessary lightness of touch. Bear in mind that the audience has no idea what you are really

4 (see p. 143)

doing. The presentation is strong enough and intriguing enough to keep their interest and is, moreover, designed to ensure that the envelope is the focal point of their attention.

Practising this trick in front of a mirror will also make you conscious of any critical angles. Obviously you don't want anyone to see the card hidden behind the envelope. One of the beauties of this trick is that it can be done in a routine along with others, or it will stand by itself and can be performed in almost any context. It is particularly strong for thinking audiences, the more intelligent they are the bigger the impact. It is a very powerful trick, one that can be categorized as intrigue magic, and the effect, as they often expressed it in old books of magic, is everything that could be desired.

HALF CUT COINCIDENCE

Here is a superb trick that will repay the minimal amount of preparation involved many times over. The unique feature of this trick is that you use thirty-four half-cards which can be easily carried in your pocket.

The Effect

'Have you ever seen anything like this before?' asks the magician. So saying, he reaches into his pocket and takes out a packet of cards encircled by an elastic band which he places on the table. The answer to his question should be no, because the packet of cards are half-cards, they have each been cut in half. Removing the elastic band, the magician offers the pack of half-cards to spectator A to shuffle **1**. When this has been done the pack is put face down on the table. Spectator A is invited to cut off a portion of the cards and spectator B is requested to pick up the remainder of the packet.

Each spectator is asked silently to count and remember the number of half-cards he is holding, while the magician turns his back. Spectator B is then instructed to hand his portion of half-cards to spectator A, who is instructed to shuffle the two packets of cards together. Then the magician turns, takes the cards and shows them one at a time to spectator A, who is asked mentally to count the cards as they are shown and to remember the particular card that falls at the number he had earlier memorized. He is told to give no visible indication of his number or the card. When the magician has finished showing each card to spectator A, he does exactly the same thing with spectator B, who also silently counts the cards as they are shown and remembers the

card that falls at his memorized number.

The magician hands the packet of cards to spectator A, who shuffles them and is instructed to look through them to find his particular card, which he is told to place face down on the table. When he has done this, spectator B follows exactly the same procedure. The magician then arranges both half-cards so that their cut edges are together, as he explains what has taken place: the packet was shuffled; each spectator had a random number of cards – only they knew how many; each number was different, and this number enabled each person to select a card in a random fashion.

The magician points to one half-card. 'This is your half, is it not?' he asks spectator A. 'And this is your half-card?' he asks spectator B, pointing to another. They agree. 'And this is more than a coincidence,' he says, turning over both half-cards to reveal that they are halves of the same card! **2** (see p. 146)

The Secret

To prepare for the trick take seventeen cards

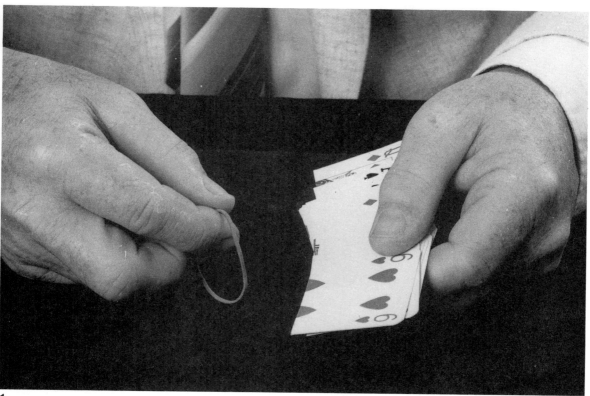

1

and cut each in half across the middle. Shuffle them, secure them with an elastic band, put the packet in your pocket and you are ready to begin.

The trick is entirely self-working with the exception of one little move which takes place when you show the cards one at a time to spectator A for him mentally to count and recall the card at the number he had memorized. The way you show the cards is as follows. Hold the cards with their faces towards spectator A in your left hand. Push off the top card with your left thumb and take it in your right hand. Then push off and show the next card, taking it in your right hand *behind* the first card. Each subsequent card is then taken and placed *behind* the card that preceded it, so you are actually reversing the order of the cards, with the *exception* of the *last* card which you keep face down in your left hand. Put all the cards in your right hand face down on top of the card in your left hand. You next proceed to show all the cards to spectator B in the same way, putting one card behind the other, but this time the last card in your left hand is put *on top* of the face-down cards in your right hand. And that's the trick. The rest is presentation. The variation in showing the cards individually is so slight that it will go completely unnoticed. Practise this trick until you have the procedure off pat and you will have added a marvellous anytime, anywhere effect to your repertoire.

2 (see p. 145)

THE CRYSTAL GAZER

This stunning trick will gain you a reputation as a magician with unusual mental powers. Read through the effect two or three times before you learn the secret. It should give you pause to consider that the methods of magic are sometimes as much a source of wonder as the miracles they produce. (This was a favourite trick of the American magician Dunninger.)

The Effect

A spectator shuffles a pack of playing-cards. The magician spreads them face down on the table in front of the spectator for him to select any card he chooses by pushing it out of the spread pack and leaving it face down on the table. The magician then puts this card into the outer breast pocket of his jacket, not letting anyone see its face, so it protrudes for half its length. The magician now displays a small crystal ball nestling in a patterned silk handkerchief. The spectator is asked to gaze into the crystal ball, clear his mind and announce what he sees. Gradually the image of a playing-card appears in the crystal. The spectator names it as the ace of hearts.

The magician reaches into his breast pocket and removes the protruding card. He shows its face to everyone. It is the ace of hearts!

The Secret

You may have to search around for a small crystal ball. Antique shops occasionally have them, and you will certainly find one in a specialist shop that deals in occult or novelty supplies. A miniature pack of cards can be purchased in a good toy shop. Having an entire pack will enable you to vary the card seen in the crystal ball in subsequent performances.

To prepare for the trick, glue a miniature ace of hearts on to the crystal ball and wrap it in your silk handkerchief. Take the ace of hearts from an ordinary pack of cards and put it into the outer breast pocket of your jacket with the face so that it cannot be seen.

Ask a spectator to shuffle the pack then ribbon spread the cards and have him push any card out of the spread. Put it into your breast pocket, pushing it down. When it is out of

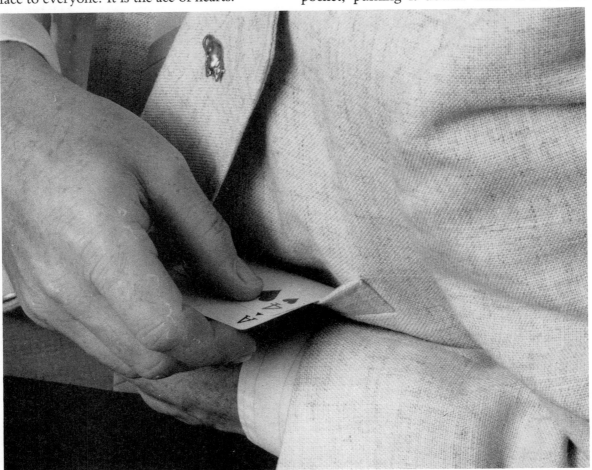

1

sight pull up the hidden ace of hearts **1** and leave about half of it showing. The face of the card should be towards your body. It should look like you have put a card into your pocket and positioned it so it can be seen. In fact you have switched one card for another. It's a simple move and a little practice in front of a mirror will show you how deceptive it can be.

When you show the spectators the crystal ball, use the silk handkerchief to polish it. This will enable you to position the ball so that the miniature card is to the side and hidden by your thumb under the silk. Anyone gazing directly down into the crystal will see nothing. Ask the spectator if he can see anything. He will answer

no. Polish the crystal again and in the process secretly turn it so that the card is on the bottom. Make him look again and he will see the image of the ace of hearts greatly magnified by the crystal **2**. Get him to name the card he sees, while you polish the ball again, turning the crystal to its original position as you do so. Show him that the image has now disappeared.

Take the card from your pocket and reveal it to be the ace of hearts. A wonderful trick!

A variation of method you might consider is to glue the miniature card to the handkerchief. This will allow you to leave the crystal ball on the table, which should be irresistible for the spectators and add to the general mystery.

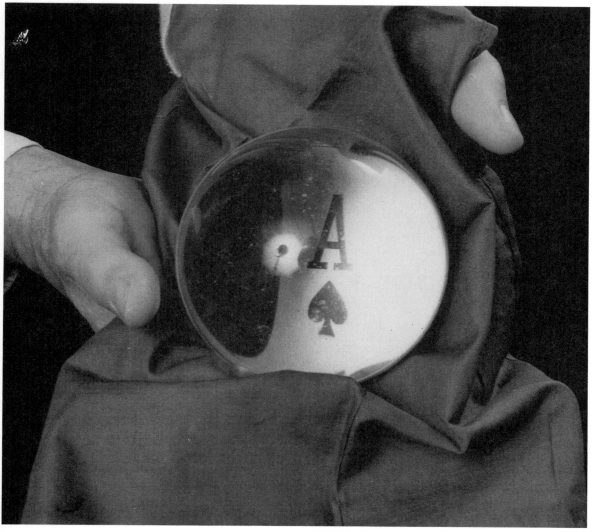

2

Telepathic Do As I Do

TELEPATHIC DO AS I DO

This trick is unusual in that most of it takes place entirely out of sight.

The Effect

Sitting opposite a spectator, the magician places two cased packs of cards on a card table. The backs should have contrasting designs or colours. Each takes a pack, removes the cards from their cases and shuffles them. The magician suggests that, given an identical set of circumstances and actions, two people thinking and doing the same thing should arrive at an identical result. The magician then proposes that every action they are about to make will take place out of sight, therefore free of unnecessary influence and distraction. He holds his pack under the table and instructs the spectator to 'do as I do'.

The spectator then holds his pack under the table. The magician shuffles his pack under the table and the spectator does the same. They exchange packs under the table. The magician shuffles this exchanged pack; the spectator does the same. The magician cuts his pack; the spectator does the same. The magician asks the spectator to take any card from his pack and hand it to the magician, who inserts it into the pack he is holding. The magician cuts his pack; the spectator does the same. The magician takes a card from his pack and gives it to the spectator, who puts it in his pack and shuffles the cards. The magician now brings his pack into view and the spectator does the same.

Both now deal cards face down in two piles on the table until both packs have been entirely dealt. During the dealing, when each came to the card with the contrasting back in their respective packs the card was put aside. When the dealing is complete, proving that there was only one contrasting card in each pack, each turn over the single cards they put aside. Both cards are identical. You will not appreciate how impressive it is until you perform it once. You will certainly keep it in your repertoire after that.

The Secret

Some advance preparation is necessary to set up the effect. Prior to performance, remove two identical cards from each pack, for example, both kings of spades. For ease of explanation and clarity we'll refer to a blue pack and a red pack. Place the blue king of spades face down on the table. On top of it place the red king of spades face down, and on top of both place the rest of the blue pack **1**. Then put the blue pack in its case. This pack now has fifty-three cards,

1 (exposed view)

2 (exposed view)

one of which is the 'stranger' red king of spades **2**. The red pack is put into its case. It has fifty-one cards. Both cases of cards are placed on the table. The magician picks up the blue pack and removes the cards. The spectator is instructed to do the same with the red pack. Both hold their packs under the table and shuffle their packs. But, before the magician shuffles his, he puts the bottom card of his pack (the blue king of spades) on his lap.

3

4

Magician and spectator now exchange packs and shuffle and cut their cards. At this point the magician secretly takes the card from his lap and adds it into his pack.

To the spectator all that seems to have happened so far is that both packs have been shuffled, then exchanged and shuffled again and cut. The reality is that the blue pack, now with the spectator, contains the red king of spades and the red pack, now with the magician, contains the blue king of spades **3**. The magician then gets the spectator to take a card from his pack and hand it to the magician, who states that he will insert it into his pack. In fact he actually places it on his lap. The magician then cuts his pack and states that he will select a card from his pack. He hands it to the spectator, who inserts it into his own pack and cuts the cards. What the magician actually does is take the card from his lap and hand it to the spectator. The spectator never dreams for a second that the card the magician gives him is the same card he gave to the magician moments earlier. All that remains to do is bring both

packs out from under the table and deal them through and reveal the identities of the cards **4**, thus proving the concept of telepathic 'do as I do.'

This is a most effective trick.

DIAL A MIRACLE

Here is a great trick that can be done without the magician and the person having the trick played on him needing to be in the same room, the same city or even the same country. Intrigued? We shall call the other person the victim – this being the term used in many old books of magic instruction for participating spectators. Given our enduring affection for the literature of magic, we felt that this blood-curdling epithet should be used for at least one of the tricks in the book.

The Effect

The magician telephones a friend and has him shuffle a pack of playing-cards and cut it into

Dial a Miracle

two approximately equal piles. He is instructed to select one pile and discard the other, then silently to count the cards in the selected pile and add together the two digits of this number but not to reveal the total to the magician. He is instructed to discard from his pile the same number of cards as the total of the two digits. Now he has to think of a number between one and ten and take that number of cards from his pile and put them in his pocket. Having done that, he is instructed to count down in the remainder of his pile to the same number and memorize the card at that position.

So far he has followed the magician's instructions and has told the magician nothing. He is now instructed to hold his selected pile of cards face down in his hand and to deal each card, singly, face up on to the table, reading out aloud the name of each card as he deals it. When he has finished, the magician immediately announces the number of cards he has in his pocket and names the selected card. Your friend – or victim – should be greatly impressed.

The Secret

This trick is another example of a powerful effect achieved by simple means. The only preparation you require is to write on a piece of paper a column of numbers from one to twenty-six. Telephone a suitable victim and instruct him as detailed under the effect. As he names each card, you write the name of each successive card against a number in sequence. For example:

1. AD
2. 3C
3. KS
4. 6D
5. 4H
6. 9H

When he has finished naming his cards, look at the number against the last card called. To take an example, we'll say it was the twelfth card. Subtract 12 from 18 (eighteen being the factor for subtraction purposes), leaving 6. The sixth card on our list is the nine of hearts and is therefore his selected card. He will have six cards in his pocket. If he calls eight cards or less,

then use 9 as the nearest subtractive factor. If he calls more than eighteen cards, then use 27 as the nearest subtractive factor.

Your victim should find this trick extremely baffling and the fact you do it long distance adds to his bewilderment.

THE LIE DETECTOR

Here is a trick that makes effective use of the concept of truthfulness to discover a spectator's selected card.

The Effect

After shuffling a pack of playing-cards the magician asks a spectator to select a card which he then commits to memory. The card is then cut back into the pack and lost. Holding the pack behind his back, the magician states that he will reverse one card in the pack that will determine the conditions under which the spectator participates in the trick. If the reversed card proves to be a red card, then the spectator must always answer truthfully the questions asked by the magician. But if the reversed card is a black card, then the spectator has the choice of answering each question truthfully or with a lie.

The magician now displays the cards from behind his back, and spreads them in his hands to find the reversed card. On locating it, he cuts the cards to bring it to the top. It is a black card. He says, 'I am now going to ask you three questions and, because the reversed card proved to be black, you have the choice of answering each question in turn with a lie or the truth.' Turning the reversed black card face down on top of the pack, the magician asks, 'Is your chosen card a red card or a black card?' If the reply is black, the magician deals one card from the top of the pack face down in a pile on the table for each letter spelt B-L-A-C-K. The second question he asks is 'Is the value of your card above seven, seven, or below seven?' Whatever the answer, the magician spells and deals one card for each letter of the answer, either A-B-O-V-E, or B-E-L-O-W or S-E-V-E-N. The final question asked is either

The Great One detecting a lie

'Was your card a club or a spade?' if the spectator had answered black to the first question, or 'Was your card a diamond or a heart?' if the spectator had answered red to the first question. Whatever the answer, the magician spells and deals one card for each letter of the suit that was named until he is holding the last card to be dealt for the last letter. He then asks the spectator not to lie but to name truthfully his selected card. He does so and the magician reveals that the card he is holding is that card.

The Secret

Prior to performing the trick you, the magician, have reversed a black card and placed it fourteenth from the bottom of the pack. Shuffling is no problem; just make sure that you only shuffle the cards overhand style above the bottom quarter of the pack so that the reversed black card remains in position fourteenth from the bottom. Spread the top half of the pack between your hands and get the spectator to select a card. Square up the pack and place it on the table. When the spectator has memorized his card, he places it face down on top of the pack, cuts the pack, completes the cut and hands you the cards. They are then held behind your back and one card is reversed in the pack – at least that's what you tell the spectator. In fact you just pretend to go through the motions of reversing a card in the pack behind your back. This bit of magical kidology enables you to display the cards and find the reversed black card fourteenth from the bottom, which you pass off as a card reversed at random. Cut the cards at this point and complete the cut, thus bringing the reversed black card to the top of the pack, and turn the black card face down on the pack. This positions the selected card fifteenth down from the top of the pack, so fifteen becomes the key number for the trick.

Questions one and two are spelt out and dealt exactly as described under the effect. But with the third question various options come into play concerning the spelling of the suit of the selected card. If the spectator had called black, then a total of ten cards will have been dealt when spelling the answer to questions one and two. Therefore there are only five cards left

of the original fifteen on top of the pack. So if C-L-U-B-S is called and dealt, the letter S will be the selected card. But if spades are called, then deal and spell S-P-A-D-E, leaving off the final S, and show the selected card on E.

However, if the spectator had called red, then eight cards would have been dealt and spelt in answer to questions one and two, leaving seven cards to reach our key number of fifteen for the last question. We handle this as follows: if hearts is called, then spell and deal H-E-A-R-T-S and the next card on top of the pack will be the selected card. If diamonds is called, then spell D-I-A-M-O-N-D, leaving off the final S, and show the selected card on D.

Although this may seem a little complicated, it really isn't, as few trial runs will prove. This is an exceptional trick that women seem to enjoy particularly. Exactly why that should be is another mystery entirely.

There is an old axiom in magic that states: never repeat a trick. It's sound advice, because very often when people are fooled, they hope to figure out the secret of a trick by seeing it again immediately. A magician, who should always be least one step ahead of his audience, can easily sidetrack them when confronted with the inevitable 'Do it again' by saying, 'I won't show you that one, but here's something you will enjoy . . .' and simply going into another trick. But audiences, particularly if they are friends and workmates whom you see regularly, can have long memories when it comes to magic, so it is more than useful to have one or two variations on the concept of a trick. Therefore here are two alternative presentations on the lie detector theme to have up your sleeve when requested at a later date to 'do that one about lying or telling the truth'

The beauty of these variations is the simplicity of method. Have a spectator shuffle a pack of cards, take them back and very casually, as you square them up, glimpse and remember the bottom card. This is your key card. Spread the cards between your hands and get them to take a card. While they look at and remember their card, square the pack again and hold it in dealing position in your left hand. Then undercut the cards by withdrawing the bottom half of the pack from your left hand so that the top half is left in dealing position. Hold out your left hand and get the spectator to replace the selected card on top of the cards and drop the cards in your right hand on to those in your left hand. This has placed your key card above the selected card. Cut the cards a couple of times and hand the pack to the spectator. Instruct the spectator to take one card at a time, look at it and name it aloud and deal it face down on to the table. At no time are you to see the face of any card. When he comes to his selected card he is to lie about its value by miscalling the name of the card and is to carry on correctly calling and dealing the remainder of the cards. Tell him that when he lies he must try not to give any indication that he's doing so either by inadvertently changing the tone of his voice or his facial expression.

The challenge is for you, the magician, to be a lie detector, even though you never see the faces of the cards. Of course all you need to do is listen for your key card to be called. Their selected card will be the next card, no matter what they miscall it as. You instantly challenge him by saying, 'I think you're lying!' And you'll be right.

The late New Yorker Paul Curry, a gifted amateur magician, came up with a clever addition that, he claimed, made this the most powerful trick he ever performed for a female spectator.

Prior to performance print in bold letters on a file or postcard the words YOU'RE A LIAR! Then hold the card so that the lettering is upside-down and facing your body and very gently bend the short ends of the card inward sufficiently to put a curve in the card which will enable it to stand on its long edge while the playing-cards are being dealt on to the table. Progress with the trick exactly as described until you hear your key card called. Then as the next card is miscalled, gently and unobtrusively blow the standing card over. The revelation of the message on the card at that moment, apparently unaided, has a terrific impact.

If you feel that the accusation 'You're a liar!' is a little too abrasive, then substitute a phrase like 'What a whopper', 'Tut tut' or 'Caught by the lie detector' or whatever you feel may be appropriate. It is important the standing card does not fall over until you want it to, so a little practice will teach you exactly how much of a curve to put in the card.

ACKNOWLEDGEMENTS

Most authors include a disclaimer in their books to the effect that, whilst they have tried to credit sources and individual creators with as much accuracy as possible, they may, inadvertently, have overlooked some appropriate acknowledgements and request forgiveness for such oversights. I have always regarded such statements with a mild degree of scepticism – until now.

The literature of magic has become so vast, and so many magicians will have contributed to the genealogy of a trick over many years, that even the most diligent and conscientious researcher must draw the line at how much valuable space is given to what threatens to be an overwhelming credit list, particularly in a book for the general public.

Every trick began with somebody, but it's amazing how few remain linked with their creator's name. Possibly this is because within the freemasonry of magic so many tricks are passed directly from one magician to another, each contributing their own variations of method and presentation. There is certainly a definitive book on the subject of reinvention in magic waiting to be written. If it ever appears it's bound to be both informative and amusing. Those who know will understand.

But I must acknowledge the great compilers of collections of magic tricks: Jean Hugard, Martin Gardner, John Scarne, Harlan Tarbell, John Northern Hilliard, Walter Gibson *et al.* who made magic accessible to me all those years ago; also that most magical source book, *Webster's Dictionary* – and, finally, Paul Daniels, who, apart from his well-known performing talents, is actually one of the most knowledgeable and practical – with all the word implies – magicians in the world.

1217